Cookin'
WILD GAME

•••••••••••••••••

The Complete Guide to Dressing and Cooking Big Game, Small Game, Upland Birds and Waterfowl

By Teresa Marrone

CREATIVE
PUBLISHING
international

MINNETONKA, MINNESOTA

www.creativepub.com

CREDITS

Creative Publishing international, Inc.
5900 Green Oak Drive
Minnetonka, MN 55343
1-800-328-3895
www.creativepub.com

President/CEO: Michael Eleftheriou
Vice President/Publisher: Linda Ball

COOKIN' WILD GAME
by Teresa Marrone

Executive Editor, Outdoor Group: David R. Maas
Senior Editor: Steven Hauge
Managing Editor: Jill Anderson
Creative Director: Brad Springer
Photo Editor: Angela Hartwell
Director of Production Services: Kim Gerber
Production Manager: Laura Hokkanen
Production Staff: Stephanie Barakos, Helga Thielen

Contibuting Photographers:
George Barnett Photography—georgebarnettphoto.com
    © George Barnett: cover top right
Sil Strung—Bozeman, Montana
    © Norm & Sil Strung: pp. 20-22 all

Printed on American paper by: R. R. Donnelley & Sons Co.
10 9 8 7 6 5 4 3 2 1

Library of Congress Cataloging-in-Publication Data

Cookin' wild game : the complete guide to dressing and cooking big game,
small game, upland birds and waterfowl.
        p. cm. -- (The Complete hunter)
    ISBN 1-58923-038-8 (soft cover)
        1. Cookery (Game) I. Complete hunter (Creative Publishing International)

TX751 .C685 2002
641.6'91--dc21   2001052999

CONTENTS

INTRODUCTION

WITH THE INCREASING AVAILABILITY OF FARM-RAISED BIRDS AND VENISON IN SUPERMARKETS AND SPECIALTY SHOPS, GAME IS ON THE MENU MORE THAN EVER. Elegant game dinners command high prices at trendy restaurants. And as the popularity of farm-raised game increases, hunters find that the truly wild game they take in the field is appreciated by more people. Unlike domestic animals, wild game has never been fed with chemicals, nor is it exposed to dangerous bacteria like so much commercial poultry and livestock. Wild game truly is a priceless treat.

But game dinners often fall short of their potential. Fearing a "wild" taste, many cooks soak the meat in saltwater and prepare it with strong seasonings that disguise the natural flavor. Or, they prepare it like domestic meat and are disappointed when it comes out tough and dry. And if the game has been handled improperly in the field, it may have an off-taste regardless of how well it is prepared.

This book will help you avoid these pitfalls. The first chapter shows you how to care for every kind of game after it's down. You'll learn how to field-dress and transport big game, and how to hang, age and skin it. The section on butchering and boning big game features complete yet concise step-by-step photos that teach you how to process your own game, assuring that you get exactly what you want from your big-game harvest.

You'll also find step-by-step directions for dressing and portioning small game, upland game birds, and waterfowl. Everything is covered, from wet- and dry-plucking birds to skinning squirrels. The chapter concludes with a comprehensive guide to freezing wild game that shows proven ways of packaging to prevent freezer burn, including techniques for water-packing game and wrapping odd-shaped cuts like ribs.

The chapter on cooking big game features more than 35 tempting recipes, including time-tested favorites such as chicken-fried venison steak, pot roast, and sausage, as well as contemporary dishes such as spicy elk kabobs and oriental-style venison ribs. Helpful how-to photos make it easy to butterfly steaks, spiral-slice a venison heart, or prepare a rolled, stuffed venison roast.

The next three chapters cover mouth-watering recipes for small game, upland birds, and waterfowl. You'll learn how to pressure-cook rabbits and squirrels so the meat is tender and delicious, as well as how to roast a goose with baked apples and barbecue partridge on a rotisserie.

The final chapter contains recipes for sauces, stuffings, and marinades to complement your game dishes. It also explains how to get the most from your game by making stock from the bones.

Every recipe in this book has been thoroughly tested by professional home economists. Dishes range in style from traditional to contemporary, but all have one thing in common: they highlight the natural, distinctive flavor of the game. Throughout the book, you'll notice icons that let you find at a glance recipes that are low-fat or are particularly quick and easy to prepare.

FAST FAST (30 to 45 minutes for preparation and cooking)

VERY FAST VERY FAST (30 minutes or less for preparation and cooking)

LOW-FAT LOW-FAT (10 or fewer grams of fat per serving)

Because wild game is harder to come by than domestic meat (and purchased farm-raised game is expensive), it pays to prepare it with the finest ingredients available. If fresh herbs are available, substitute them for the dried herbs listed; simply double the amount and add them near the end of the cooking time. And when a recipe calls for wine, use a good table wine. If you prefer to make the recipes non-alcoholic, use broth or water instead.

Read through this book before your next hunt, then refer to it in seasons to come to ensure that you make the most of your wild harvest. The savory game dishes you prepare will be as memorable as the hunts that made them possible.

1

FIELD-
DRESSING

WILD GAME

Big Game: Field-Dressing & Transport

A little homework before a big-game hunt can save a lot of time and effort once you've bagged your animal. And it will ensure that the meat you bring home will be in prime condition for the table.

Familiarize yourself with state and local regulations. Some states prohibit quartering and skinning in the field; others require that you turn in certain parts for biological study. Be sure to check the regulations booklet available with your license. For more information, contact state or federal wildlife-management agencies.

If you are hunting for a trophy, consult in advance with a reliable taxidermist. He can give you advice on the best ways to handle the head and antlers in the field. There are also several good do-it-yourself kits for antler mounting and hide tanning.

The hides of deer, moose, and elk make excellent leather. Many tanneries will buy raw hides directly from hunters. If you plan on selling the hide, find out how the buyer wants it prepared. Some tanneries will exchange a raw hide for a pair of finished leather gloves. Or, you may want to have the hide tanned and returned to you.

Unless you have a reliable cold-storage area for holding your animal prior to butchering, make arrangements with a locker plant before you hunt. Ask about the locker's business hours; you don't want to return from hunting on a warm Saturday only to discover the plant is closed for the weekend.

HANG field-dressed big game in a tree to speed its cooling. Hanging also helps protect it from scavenging animals if you must leave to get help carrying it out. Use a block and tackle (inset) for easier lifting.

SELECTING & SHARPENING HUNTING KNIVES

A good hunting knife is one of the best investments a hunter can make. Properly selected, used, and cared for, it may well outlive him. A cheap knife, on the other hand, may not last a single hunting season.

When selecting a hunting knife, look closely at the materials, blade length and shape, and workmanship.

The blade steel should be stainless, hard but not brittle. A blade with a Rockwell hardness rating of 57 to 60 is hard enough to hold an edge, but soft enough for easy resharpening at home when it does become dull.

The handle should be made of hardwood, plastic-impregnated wood, or a tough synthetic. These materials last longer than brittle plastic, or than wood you can easily dent with your fingernail.

Select a knife that feels comfortable in your hand. Remember that your hands may be wet when you're using it, and look for a handle shape that's easy to hold firmly. A blade between 3½ and 4½ inches long is adequate for either big or small game.

Clip-point and drop-point knives are good all-purpose types. The acutely pointed tip of a clip-point is good for delicate cutting, and penetrates the abdominal skin easily in field-dressing. The tip of a drop-point is less apt to puncture the intestines when slitting the abdominal skin, or to punch a hole in the hide should you use it for skinning.

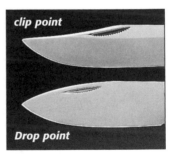

For convenience and safety in the field, many hunters prefer folding knives. They are shorter and easier to carry than a straight knife, and the folded blade is safely out of the way in the event of a fall. Choose folding knives carefully, checking for quality construction. When fully opened, the blade should lock in position with no trace of wiggle or sloppiness, and the back of the blade should line up exactly with the back edge of the handle. A folding combination knife eliminates the need for multiple tools. Many contain a blunt-tip blade for slitting abdomens without puncturing intestines, a clip-point blade, and a saw for cutting through the breastbones and pelvic bones of big game.

Use your knife only for its intended purpose. If you use it to hack wood or pry the lid off a jar, you could destroy the edge. Be sure your knife is clean and dry before you store it at the end of the season. Over time, even modern stainless steel can be corroded by salts or acids.

A sharp blade is safer than a dull one. It gives you more control, and you need less pressure to get the job done. Dress the edge often with a sharpening steel. A steel does not remove metal from the blade, but simply realigns the edge. When the blade becomes so dull that the steel won't dress it, sharpen it with a whetstone.

How to Sharpen a Knife

SELECT a medium whetstone at least as long as the blade. (If the blade is extremely dull, use a coarse stone first, then the medium stone.) Place the stone on a folded towel for stability, and apply a little honing oil.

HOLD the base of the blade against the whetstone at the angle at which the blade was originally sharpened (usually between 12 and 17 degrees). Using moderate pressure, push the knife away from you in a smooth arc from base to tip, as if shaving thin pieces off the face of the stone. Keep the edge of the blade at the same angle, in constant contact with the whetstone. Repeat this pushing motion two more times.

TURN the knife over and draw it toward you in an arc three times, maintaining the same angle. Continue sharpening alternate sides, adding oil if necessary, until the blade hangs up when drawn very gently over a fingernail.

REPEAT the previous steps on a fine whetstone. If the stone clogs, wipe and re-oil it. The knife is sharp when it slices effortlessly through a piece of paper. Clean the whetstone with soapy water for storage.

IN THE FIELD

Before you shoot, consider the location and body position of the animal. Remember that you'll have to get it out of the area after it's down. If you spot an animal across a canyon, consider possible drag routes before shooting. A moose standing in a bog may be a tempting target, but you would probably need several people to move it to dry land for field-dressing and quartering.

Shot placement affects both the quality and quantity of the meat you bring home. A study at Texas A&M University showed that game killed instantly with a clean shot produces meat more tender and flavorful than game only wounded with the first shot. Game animals, like humans, produce adrenaline and other chemicals when frightened or stressed. These chemicals make the meat tough and gamey. A poorly placed shot may also damage choice cuts, or rupture the stomach or intestines, tainting the meat.

If possible, shoot an animal that's standing still rather than running. A shot in the heart or neck will drop it instantly, and you'll lose little meat.

Approach a downed animal with caution, keeping your gun loaded and staying away from the hooves and antlers. Nudge the animal with your foot, or gently touch your gun barrel to its eye. If there's any reaction, shoot it in the head or heart. When certain the animal is dead, unload your gun

QUICK TIP: Some common items for field-dressing include a folding lock-back knife and a spare; a small whetstone; several foot-long pieces of kitchen string; 2 clean sponges; zip-lock plastic bags; rubber gloves; block and tackle; and 20 feet of 1/4-inch rope. If hunting moose or elk, also bring cloth bags for carrying out the quarters if skinned, and a belt axe or folding saw for quartering. Hooks can be slipped over the edges of the split ribcage, then tied to trees to hold the body open while gutting. Stow everything but the belt axe in your pack, along with a first-aid kit and other hunting gear.

and place it safely out of the way.

As you field-dress the animal, look for parasites, tumors, growths or spots on internal organs which could indicate a disease. Most of these deer are safe to handle and eat; if in doubt, contact a wildlife professional.

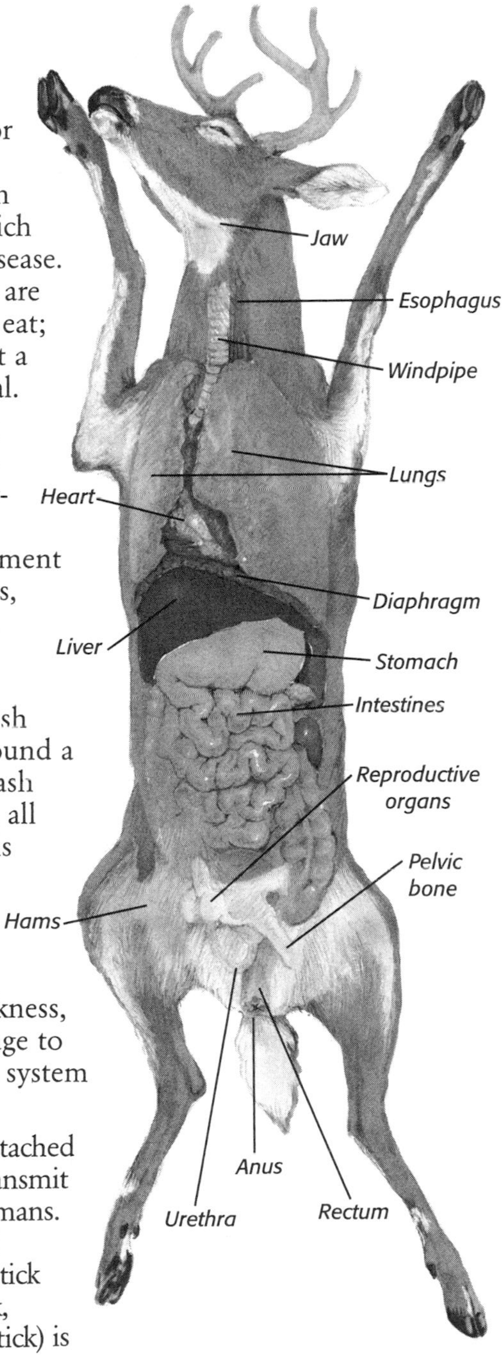

One common and potentially dangerous affliction, however, is Lyme disease, a bacterial ailment that affects humans, dogs and livestock. The first sign of Lyme disease is often a large, reddish rash that forms around a tick bite. But the rash does not appear in all cases. The disease is easily treated in this early stage, but if allowed to advance, it may cause extreme weakness, paralysis and damage to the joints, nervous system and heart.

Some of the ticks attached to big game may transmit Lyme disease to humans. In the Midwest and Northeast, the deer tick (also called bear tick, sheep tick or Lyme tick) is

Jaw

Esophagus

Windpipe

Lungs

Heart

Diaphragm

Liver

Stomach

Intestines

Reproductive organs

Pelvic bone

Hams

Anus

Urethra

Rectum

the major culprit. In the Southeast, the black-legged tick is the suspected carrier. Recently, researchers have discovered that several other species of ticks and biting insects such as flies and mosquitos can also carry Lyme disease.

CAUTION: Major carriers of Lyme disease are deer ticks, both the female and nymph. Black-legged ticks may transmit the disease in the Southeast; they're almost identical to deer ticks. The common dog tick, which is much larger, occasionally carries the disease.

You can reduce the chances of getting a tick bite by treating exposed skin and clothing with DEET-based insect repellent. But the best protection is permethrin, which is applied to clothing but not exposed skin. It kills ticks that crawl across the fabric.

Wear rubber gloves when you field-dress big game, and don't cut yourself; infected game blood in contact with an open wound could transmit the disease.

The step-by-step instructions on the following pages will guide you through a field-dressing procedure that produces a clean carcass. Splitting the pelvis is optional with this method. In warm weather, you may wish to split the pelvis, because the hams cool faster when separated. However, an animal with a split pelvis is more difficult to drag. The separated hind legs flop around, and the cavity may get dirty.

If you elect to split the pelvis, cut between the hams as described. Then, locate the natural seam between the two halves of the pelvic bone and cut through it with your knife. On a large or old animal, you may need to use a game saw or hatchet. Some hunters stand their knife upright with its tip on the seam, then strike the knife with their palm to split the pelvis. Do not attempt this unless you have a sturdy knife; you could damage the blade.

Be sure to follow state regulations requiring evidence of the sex left on the carcass. Antlers are usually adequate to identify a buck; in some states, antlers must be a certain length for the animal to be legal.

Where the law allows, attach the registration tag after field-dressing, rather than before. The tag may get ripped off during the dressing procedure.

HOW TO FIELD-DRESS A DEER (directions for a right-handed hunter)

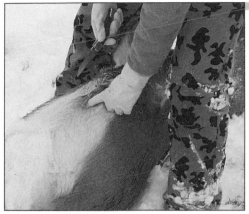

1. RUN your finger along the breastbone until you can feel the end of it. Pinch the skin away from the body so you don't puncture the intestines, and then make a shallow cut just long enough to insert the first two fingers of your left hand.

2. FORM a V with your first two fingers, maintaining upward pressure. Guide the blade between your fingers with the cutting edge up; this way, you won't cut into the intestines. Cut through the abdominal wall back to the pelvic area.

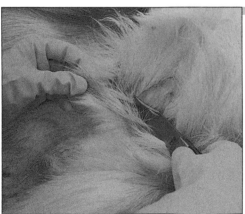

3. SEPARATE the external reproductive organs of a buck from the abdominal wall, but do not cut them off completely. Remove the udder of a doe if she was still nursing. The milk sours rapidly and could give the meat an unpleasant flavor.

HOW TO FIELD-DRESS A DEER (continued)

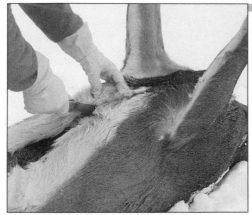

4. STRADDLE the animal, facing its head. Unless you plan to mount the head, cut the skin from the base of the breastbone to the jaw, with the cutting edge of the knife up. If you plan to mount the head, skip this step and the next.

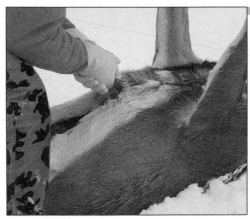

5. BRACE your elbows against your legs, with your left hand supporting your right. Cut through the center of the breastbone, using your knees to provide leverage. If the animal is old or very large, you may need to use a game saw or small axe.

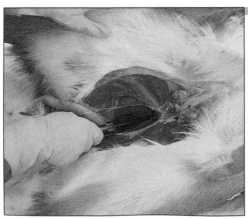

6. SLICE between the hams to free a buck's urethra, or if you elect to split the pelvic bone on either a buck or doe. Make careful cuts around the urethra until it is freed to a point just above the anus. Be careful not to sever the urethra.

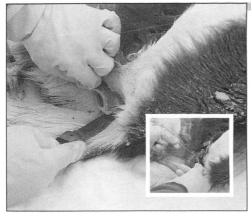

7. CUT around the anus; on a doe, the cut should also include the reproductive opening (above the anus). Free the rectum and urethra by loosening the connective tissue with your knife. Tie off the rectum and urethra with kitchen string (inset).

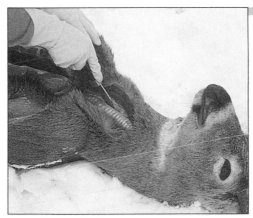

8. FREE the windpipe and esophagus by cutting the connective tissue; sever them at the jaw. Grasp them firmly and pull down, continuing to cut where necessary, until they're freed to the point where the windpipe branches out into the lungs.

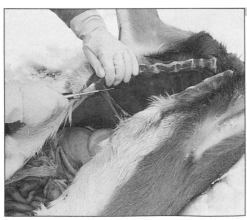

9. HOLD the rib cage open on one side with your left hand. Cut the diaphragm from the rib opening down to the backbone. Stay as close to the rib cage as possible; do not puncture the stomach. Repeat on the other side so the cuts meet over the backbone.

HOW TO FIELD-DRESS A DEER (continued)

10. PULL the tied-off rectum and urethra underneath the pelvic bone and into the body cavity, unless you have split the pelvic bone. If so, this is unnecessary. Roll the animal on its side so the entrails begin to spill out of the body cavity.

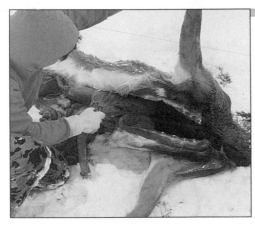

11. GRASP the windpipe and esophagus; pull down and away from the body. If the organs do not pull freely away, the diaphragm may still be attached. Scoop from both ends toward the middle to finish rolling out the entrails. Detach the heart and liver.

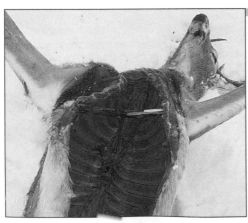

12. PROP the body cavity open with a stick after sponging the cavity clean. If the urinary tract or intestines have been severed, wash the meat with snow or clean water. Hang the carcass from a tree to speed cooling, or drape it over brush or logs with the body cavity down.

TRANSPORTING BIG-GAME ANIMALS

After field-dressing, move the animal to camp as soon as possible. Leave the hide on to protect the meat from dirt and flies. The hide also prevents the surface from drying too much during aging. In hot weather, however, you may want to remove the hide in the field to cool the carcass.

If you plan to skin the animal in the field, bring along a large cloth bag or sheet to keep the meat clean during transport. Never put the carcass or quarters in plastic bags unless the meat is thoroughly chilled. The plastic traps the body heat, and the meat may be ruined. Avoid plastic garbage bags; they may be treated with a toxic disinfectant.

You may have to quarter an elk or moose to transport it from the field (pages 20-22). Some hunters skin the animal before quartering, so the hide can be tanned in one piece. Others prefer to quarter the animal first. A quartered hide is still suitable for tanning; in fact, most tanneries split whole elk or moose hides in half to make them easier to handle.

For safety reasons, wear blaze-orange clothing when you move an animal in the field. The traditional method of carrying a deer, by lashing it to a pole between two hunters, is not recommended. If you must carry an animal this way, drape it completely with blaze-orange cloth.

Once in camp, hang the animal up. Hanging aids cooling and blood drainage, and the stretching helps tenderize the meat. Clean the clots and excess blood from the heart and liver, then place the organs in plastic bags on ice.

Ideally, the carcass should be cooled to 40°F within 24 hours. Cool it as rapidly as possible, but don't allow it to freeze. The meat loses moisture if frozen and thawed, and the carcass is difficult to skin when frozen even partially. If the days are warm and the nights cool, keep the carcass covered with a sleeping bag during the day. If the nights are warm as well, store the carcass at a locker plant.

The best way to transport the animal home is in a closed trailer or covered pickup. If your trip is long and hot, pack bags of dry ice around the carcass. Or, quarter the animal, wrap well in plastic, and pack it into coolers with ice. Be sure to check state laws regarding transport of big game.

HOW TO QUARTER AN ELK

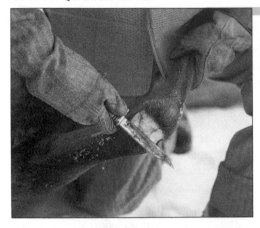

1. BEND a leg sharply, then cut the skin around the joint to remove the lower leg. Repeat on all legs.

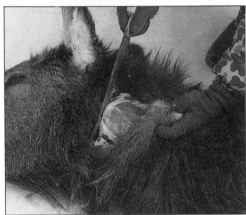

2. SAW off the head after skinning the neck area. Sawing it before skinning would force hair into the meat.

3. CUT between the third and fourth ribs, from the backbone to the tips of the ribs. Cut from inside the body.

4. SEPARATE the front half of the animal from the rear half by sawing through the backbone.

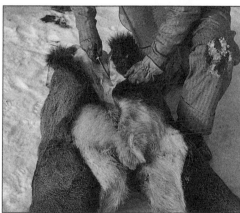

5. SPLIT the hide along the backbone on both halves, then peel it back several inches on each side of the cut.

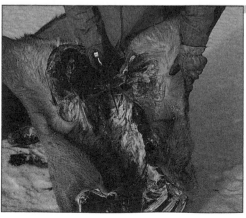

6. PROP one half against your legs, then begin sawing lengthwise through the backbone.

HOW TO QUARTER AN ELK (continued)

7. CONTINUE cutting while keeping the back off the ground. Gravity will help pull the quarters apart, making the cutting easier. Your saw will not bind, as it would if the half were lying on the ground.

8. A QUARTERED elk looks like this. Depending on the animal's size, elk quarters weigh 60 to 125 pounds each. Where the law allows, some hunters bone the animal in the field to reduce weight.

9. DRAG out a hindquarter by punching a hole behind the last rib, then threading a rope through and tying as pictured. This way, you drag with the grain of the hair. To drag out a forequarter, tie a rope tightly around the neck.

Hanging, Aging & Skinning Big Game

How should I hang my animal – from the head or by the hind legs? And what about aging – does it improve the meat or spoil it? If I'm going to age the animal, should I leave the hide on or take it off? These questions cause a great deal of debate among hunters.

If you want the head for a trophy, the first question is answered for you: the animal must be hung by the hind legs. Many hunters hang all big game this way, and the U.S. Department of Agriculture recommends this method for butchering beef. Hanging by the hind legs allows the blood to drain from the choice hindquarters. If your animal must be hung outdoors, however, it's better to hang it from the head because of the direction of hair growth. Otherwise, the upturned hair would trap rain and snow.

Many laboratory and taste tests have demonstrated that aging will definitely tenderize the meat. The special tenderness and flavor of beef prime rib result from extended aging. Wild game can benefit in the same way. It's a matter of personal taste: some prefer the aged flavor and tenderness, others don't. Aging is unnecessary if all the meat will be ground into sausage or burger.

To prevent unwanted bacterial growth during the aging process, the carcass temperature must be stabilized between 35° and 40°F. If it fluctuates widely, condensation may form. Temperatures above 40° promote excess bacterial growth and cause the fat to turn rancid. If you age the animal outdoors or in a shed, be prepared to butcher it immediately or take it to a locker should the weather turn warm.

Leave the hide on during aging, if possible. It helps stabilize the temperature of the meat and also reduces dehydration. In a study at the University of Wyoming, an elk carcass was cut in half down the backbone; one half was skinned, the other was not. After two weeks of aging, the skinned side lost over 20 percent more moisture. Animals aged without the hide will have a great deal of dried, dark meat to be trimmed, further reducing your yield.

During aging, enzyme activity breaks down the connective tissue that makes meat tough. Elk has more connective tissue than deer, antelope, or bear, and can be aged longer. Antelope is probably the most tender of these animals; extended aging may give it a mushy texture. Many people prefer their antelope aged only about 3 days. Bear can age from 3 days to a week. Deer and cow elk reach their prime in a week to 10 days, and bull elk require up to 14 days. These times are for ideal conditions. Do not attempt to age an animal in warm conditions.

Some people prefer to quarter their meat, wrap the quarters in cloth, then age them in a refrigerator or old chest-style pop cooler. The effects are almost the same as hanging a whole carcass. The meat may be slightly less tender, because it doesn't get stretched as much.

If you prefer not to age the animal, delay butchering for at least 24 hours, until the carcass has cooled and the muscles have relaxed. The cuts will be ragged and unappealing if you start before cooling is complete, and the meat will be tough if butchered while the muscles are still contracted.

SKINNING BIG GAME

Skinning is easiest while the animal is still warm. If you age the meat, however, it's best to leave the skin on until butchering.

Most hunters skin their animals by hand. The task isn't difficult, requiring only a knife and a saw. For easiest skinning, hang the animal from a pulley. Then you can raise or lower the carcass so the area you're working on will always be at eye level. Or, hoist the animal on a rope running through a heavy-duty screw eye fastened to a solid ceiling beam.

Try to keep hair off the meat during skinning. Keep your knife sharp, touching it up as necessary with a steel or stone. Cut through the skin from the inside out, so your knife slips between the hairs. This way, you avoid cutting hairs in half or driving them into the meat, and your knife won't dull as quickly.

After skinning, lay the hide out on a piece of plywood, skin side up. If you take a few moments to scrape off any bits of meat or fat, you will get a better piece of leather.

Most tanneries prefer to receive a hide salted and rolled. To protect it from rain and animals during the salting process, find a sheltered spot like a shed or garage. Sprinkle the skin side liberally with salt, and rub some into the edges, cuffs, and neck area. Tilt the plywood slightly so the hide will drain.

After a day, add more salt and fold the hide in half, skin side in. Roll the folded hide into a bundle and tie it with twine. Don't put the rolled hide in plastic, except for shipping, because it may rot. Keep it cold, and get it to the tannery as soon as possible.

If you have a deer hide, save the tail. It can be used for jig and fly tying, and hide buyers may pay several dollars for it.

If you're not going to butcher the animal yourself, deliver the carcass to the butcher with the hide still on, and let him skin it.

TOOLS for skinning big game include: (1) bone saw; (2) small knife for close trimming; (3) curved-blade skinning knife; and (4) knife sharpener.

HOW TO SKIN AN ANIMAL HANGING BY THE HIND LEGS *(pictured: Deer)*

1. PEEL the skin over the hind leg to uncover the large tendon at the back of the leg. Carefully slit any tissue between the bone and the large tendon. Place the end of the gambrel into the area between the leg bone and tendon, and hoist the carcass to a comfortable height.

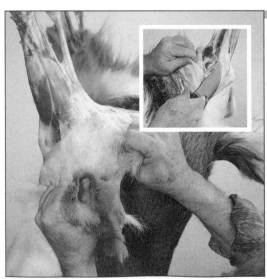

2. CUT the hide along the inner side of each hind leg with the knife blade turned away from the carcass. Rotate the knife blade back toward the meat (inset) and begin skinning the hide around the leg. Pull on the hide with your hands once you reach the outside of each leg.

3. PULL the remaining hide down the outside of each leg until the skinned part reaches the tail. Sever the tail close to the deer's rump, leaving the tailbone inside the hide (left). Continue skinning down the deer's back by loosening the hide with your knife.

4. PULL the hide down the deer's back with your hands (left). Use your knife only where necessary, and take care not to cut a hole in the hide. Continue peeling down the deer's back and around the rib cage until you reach the front shoulders.

HOW TO SKIN AN ANIMAL HANGING BY THE HIND LEGS (continued)

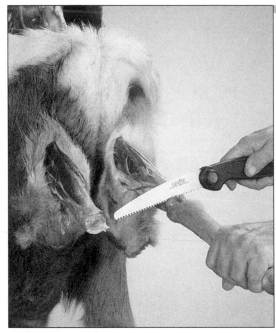

5. CUT with your knife along the inside of each front leg and peel the hide off the front legs just as you did with the hind legs. Saw off the front legs just above the joint (left). Peel the hide from the brisket and over the deer's shoulders.

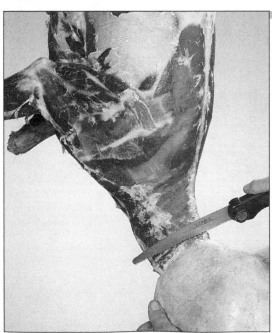

6. CONTINUE peeling the hide down the neck as far as possible. Saw off the head at the base of the skull (left). After skinning, lay the hide out on a flat surface, scrape off any bits of meat or fat, and salt the hide.

Butchering Big Game

When you do your own butchering, you know that the meat has been handled with care, and you get the cuts you prefer. You will probably be willing to take more time trimming than a butcher would, so your finished cuts may have less gristle, fat, and silverskin on them. Equipment needed for butchering includes a hunting or boning knife, sharpening steel or whetstone, heavy-duty plastic wrap, freezer paper, freezer tape, waterproof marking pen, game or meat saw and a kitchen scale.

In most cases, the animal is butchered while still hanging from the skinning process. Use caution when butchering a hanging animal. When you cut off each portion, you must "catch" it, and this can be tricky with a knife in one hand. A deer leg, for instance, may weigh 20 pounds or more, so you may need a partner to catch it. Be absolutely certain that your partner stays clear of your knife, and never allow him to cut at the same time. For safety, some hunters prefer to butcher on a large table.

The photo sequence on pages 32 to 35 shows how to cut up a deer that is hanging from the head. The procedure is somewhat different if the animal is hanging by the hind legs. You will not be able to cut off the hind legs because they are supporting the carcass. Instead, remove the front legs, backstrap, and ribs as described, then place the hindquarters on a table to finish cutting.

After cutting up the carcass, bone the meat. Boning is easier than bone-in butchering and usually results in tastier meat. Bone marrow is fatty and can turn rancid, even in the freezer. By boning, you avoid cutting the bones, so there is no bone residue to affect the meat's flavor. In addition, boned meat takes less freezer space and is easier to wrap. There are no sharp edges to puncture the freezer wrap and expose the meat to freezer burn.

On pages 36 to 39, you'll learn an easy method for boning a big-game animal. To roughly estimate the amount of boned meat you will get, divide the field-dressed weight of your animal in half. You will get a smaller yield if the shot damaged much meat, or if you aged the animal.

Work on a large hardwood or plexiglass cutting board. To keep bacterial growth to a minimum, wash the board with a solution of 3 tablespoons of household bleach to 1 gallon of water, and wash it occasionally during the boning process. Keep two large bowls handy for the trimmings. As you bone, place large chunks to be used for stew in one bowl; small scraps for sausage or burger in the other.

How you make the final boning cuts depends on the animal's size. On a moose, for instance, the rump portion is large enough to yield several roasts. But on an antelope, the same cut is too small for a roast, and is better for steaks, kabobs, or stroganoff.

Keep the meat cool throughout the butchering and boning process. Work on the carcass in a cool shed or garage. To reduce bacterial growth, bone and freeze each portion as you remove it, or refrigerate it until you can bone it. You can butcher faster by working in pairs; while one person cuts up the carcass, the other works on boning.

Save the bones if you want to make soup or stock (page 175). The backbone makes particularly good stock. Saw the larger bones into pieces to fit your stockpot.

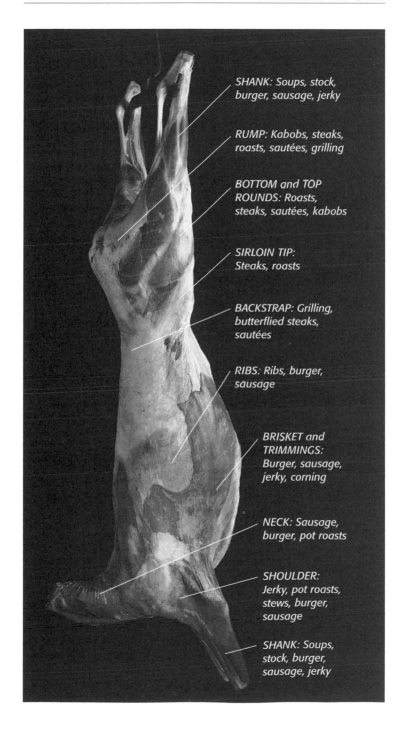

SHANK: Soups, stock, burger, sausage, jerky

RUMP: Kabobs, steaks, roasts, sautées, grilling

BOTTOM and TOP ROUNDS: Roasts, steaks, sautées, kabobs

SIRLOIN TIP: Steaks, roasts

BACKSTRAP: Grilling, butterflied steaks, sautées

RIBS: Ribs, burger, sausage

BRISKET and TRIMMINGS: Burger, sausage, jerky, corning

NECK: Sausage, burger, pot roasts

SHOULDER: Jerky, pot roasts, stews, burger, sausage

SHANK: Soups, stock, burger, sausage, jerky

HOW TO CUT UP A BIG-GAME ANIMAL *(pictured: Deer)*

1. PUSH the front leg away from the body, then begin cutting between the leg and the rib cage. Continue until you reach the shoulder. It helps to have someone steady the carcass, but make sure he or she is safely away from your knife.

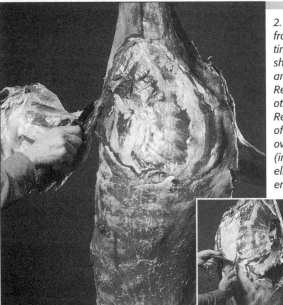

2. REMOVE the front leg by cutting between the shoulder blade and the back. Repeat with the other leg. Remove the layer of brisket meat over the ribs (inset). Moose or elk brisket is thick enough to be rolled for corning. Grind thin brisket for burger.

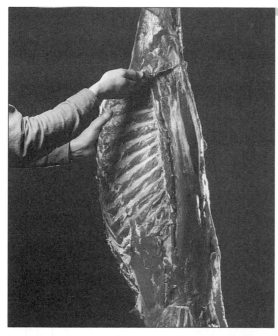

3. CUT the meat at the base of the neck to begin removing a backstrap. There are two backstraps, one on each side of the spine. Backstraps can be butterflied for steaks (page 79), cut into roasts, or sliced thinly for sautéeing. The lower part, or loin, is most tender.

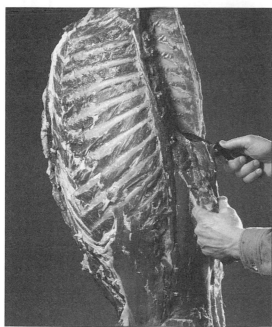

4. MAKE two cuts between the shoulder and rump: one along the spine, the other along the rib tops. Keep your knife close to the bones, removing as much meat as possible. Cut off this first backstrap at the rump, then remove the backstrap on the other side of the spine.

HOW TO CUT UP A BIG-GAME ANIMAL (continued)

5. BEGIN cutting one hind leg away, exposing the ball-and-socket joint (arrow). Push the leg back to pop the joint apart, then cut through the joint. Work your knife around the tailbone and pelvis until the leg is removed. Repeat with the other leg.

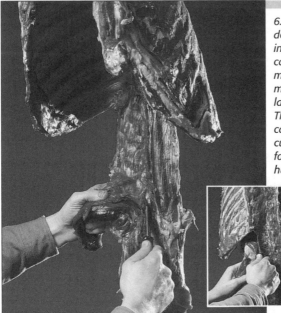

6. CUT the tenderloins from inside the body cavity after trimming the flank meat below the last rib (inset). The flank meat can be ground, or cut into thin strips for jerky. Many hunters remove the tenderloins before aging the animal, to keep them from darkening and dehydrating.

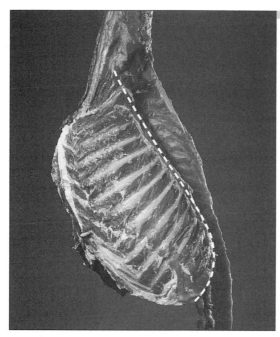

7. REMOVE the ribs, if desired, by sawing along the backbone (dotted lines). Cut around the base of the neck, then twist the backbone off. Separate the neck and head (page 28). Bone the neck to grind for burger, or keep it whole for pot roasting.

8. TRIM the ribs by cutting away the ridge of meat and gristle along the bottom. If the ribs are long, saw them in half. Cut ribs into racks of three or four. If you don't want to save the ribs, you can bone the meat between them and grind it for burger or sausage.

HOW TO BONE A HIND LEG (pictured: Antelope)

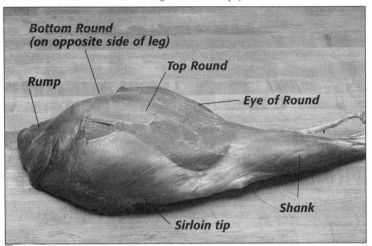

1. A HIND LEG consists of the sirloin tip, the top and bottom rounds, the eye of round, a portion of the rump, and the shank. The sirloin, rounds, and rump are tender cuts for roasting or grilling; the shank is tough, and best for ground meat or soups.

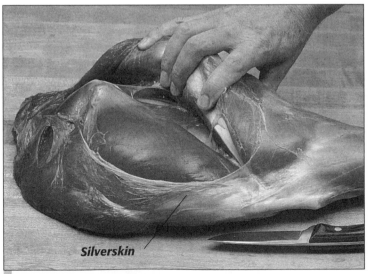

2. SEPARATE the top round from the rest of the leg after cutting through the thin layer of silverskin that covers the leg. Work your fingers into the natural seam, then begin pulling the top round away from the leg. Use your knife only where necessary to free the meat.

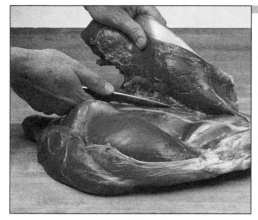

3. CUT along the back of the leg to remove the top round completely. The top round is excellent when butterflied, rolled and tied for roasting (pages 40-41). Or, cut it into two smaller flat roasts, cube for kabobs, or slice for sautées.

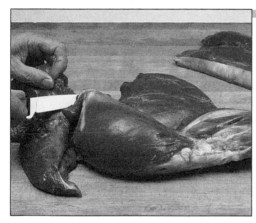

4. REMOVE the rump portion. Cut the rump off at the top of the hipbone after removing the silverskin and pulling the muscle groups apart with your fingers. A large rump is excellent for roasting; a small one can be cut for steaks, kabobs, or sautées.

5. CUT bottom round away from sirloin tip after turning leg over and separating these two muscle groups with your fingers. Next, carve sirloin tip away from bone. Sirloin tip makes a choice roast or steaks; bottom round is good for roasting, steaks, or kabobs.

HOW TO BONE A HIND LEG (continued)

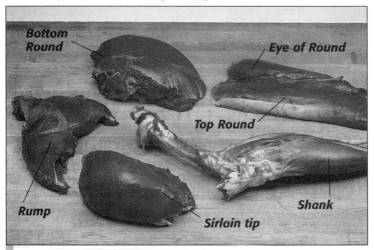

6. A BONED LEG will look like this. Cut the shank and upper leg bone apart at the knee joint if you plan on using the shank for soup. Or, cut the meat off the shank close to the bone; trim away the tendons and silverskin, and grind the meat for burger or sausage. Use the leftover bones for stock (page 175). On a larger animal, you may wish to separate the eye of round from the top round.

7. MAKE large-diameter steaks from a whole hind leg by cutting across all the muscle groups rather than boning as described above. First, remove the rump portion as described, then cut the leg into inch-thick steaks. As each steak is cut, work around the bone with a fillet knife, then slide the steak over the end of the bone. Continue steaking until you reach the shank.

HOW TO BONE A FRONT LEG (pictured: Deer)

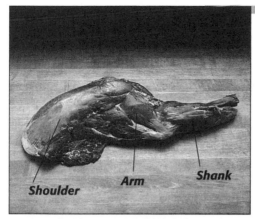

Shoulder **Arm** **Shank**

1. A FRONT LEG consists of the shoulder, arm, and shank. The meat from the front leg is less tender than that from the hind leg, and is used for pot roasting, stews, jerky, or grinding.

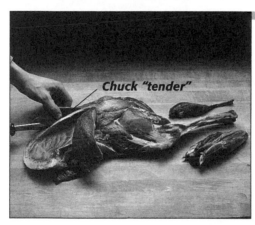

Chuck "tender"

2. CUT along bony ridge in the middle of the shoulder blade. One side yields the small boneless chuck "tender." Bone the other side along the dotted line to make a shoulder roast.

Chuck "tender" **Shank meat** **Shoulder roast**

3. TRIM remaining meat from bones. Use the chuck "tender" for jerky or stews. Pot roast the shoulder roast, cut into stew chunks, or use for jerky. Grind the shank meat for burger.

HOW TO MAKE A ROLLED ROAST *(pictured: Deer Bottom Round)*

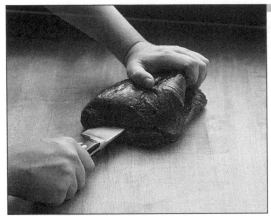

1. BUTTERFLY meat that is thicker than one inch by cutting into two thinner pieces; leave the meat connected at one edge. Open the butterflied meat up so it lies flat. Roll the meat tightly with the grain, tucking in any irregular edges.

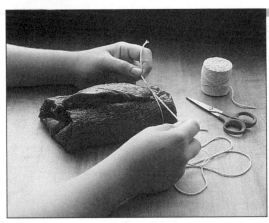

2. TIE the rolled meat about an inch from the end that is farthest from you; use a 60" length of kitchen string. Leave several inches at the short end of the string; you will need to tie the two ends of the string together after making loops around the meat.

3. MAKE a loop in the string, then twist the loop once to make a small "braid" (arrow). Slip the braided loop over the end of the meat closest to you, then slide the loop so it is about one inch from the string tied around the far end.

4. SNUG up this first loop by pulling on the long end of the string, adjusting its length so the braid lines up with the original knot. The roast will look more attractive when it is served if all the braids are lined up along the top of the roast.

5. CONTINUE making loops about an inch apart, snugging them up as you go. Tie on additional string if necessary. When you have made a loop about an inch from the close end (dotted line), slip the string underneath the roast so it comes out on the far side.

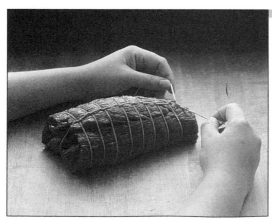

6. TIE the two ends of the string together with a double overhand knot. Trim both ends of the string close to the knot. When you are ready to carve a cooked rolled roast, simply snip the loops along the top of the roast and pull off the string.

Dressing Small Game

Proper field care of small game ensures excellent eating. Field-dress rabbits, hares, and squirrels as soon as possible, or the delicately flavored meat may pick up an unpleasant taste. Squirrel seems particularly susceptible to off-tastes, so knowledgeable hunters take time to field-dress squirrels immediately after shooting.

A great deal has been written about small game transmitting diseases to humans. Such diseases are contracted by handling entrails or uncooked meat from infected animals. Bacteria passes through cuts in a person's skin or through the mucous membranes. But infected animals are rarely encountered, because the diseases usually kill them or weaken them so much that predators can easily capture them.

To avoid any danger, never shoot an animal that moves erratically or otherwise appears sick. Wear rubber gloves when dressing or skinning any small game. Never touch your mouth or eyes, and wash your hands thoroughly when finished. Dispose of the entrails and skin in a spot where dogs and cats can't reach them and become infected. For safer disposal, some hunters carry plastic bags.

When field-dressing small game, you may encounter various internal parasites. Most of these, while visually unappealing, do not harm the meat and are removed during dressing or skinning.

When handling rabbits, wear the gloves not only for dressing and skinning, but also during all stages of kitchen preparation. Rabbits occasionally carry tularemia, a bacterial disease that can be transmitted to humans. Thorough cooking destroys the bacteria.

After dressing, small-game animals must be cooled properly. Don't put them in a hot car or carry them for hours in the pocket of your hunting coat. Instead, leave them in a shaded spot, out of the reach of predators. Some hunters hang their field-dressed animals in a shady tree, so the carcasses can drain as well as cool. Never put an animal in a plastic bag until it's completely cooled.

In warm weather, it's best to chill the dressed animals in a cooler. Reusable plastic ice packs are better than plain ice, since they won't fill the cooler with melted water. Plastic soda bottles filled with water and then frozen also work well.

Before skinning, try to determine the animal's age, because this may affect the way you cook it. The tail of a young squirrel tapers to a point, while the tail of an old one is the same width throughout. A young rabbit has soft, flexible ears and a small cleft in the upper lip; an old one has stiffer ears, often with white edges, and a deeply cleft upper lip. In all kinds of small game, the meat of old animals is darker in color. Also, the teeth darken and dull with age, and the claws become blunt.

HOW TO FIELD-DRESS SMALL GAME

MAKE a shallow cut (dotted line) from the vent to the rib cage with a small hunting knife. Be sure not to puncture the intestines. Some hunters extend the cut through the rib cage to the neck.

PULL OUT all the entrails. Check a rabbit's liver for white spots indicating disease; if it's clean, save it in a plastic bag with the heart. Wipe cavity with paper towels.

HOW TO SKIN A RABBIT OR HARE

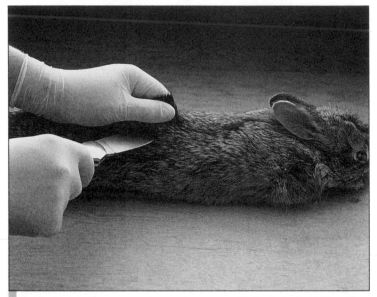

1. PINCH the hide up and away from the middle of the rabbit's spine. Slit the hide from the spine down the sides, being careful not to cut the meat.

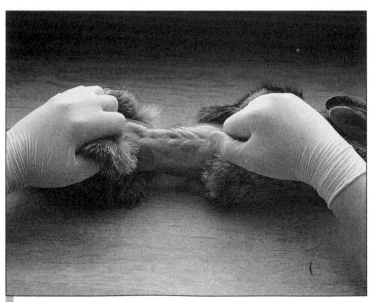

2. GRASP the hide with both hands and pull in opposite directions. Keep pulling until all the legs are skinned up to the feet.

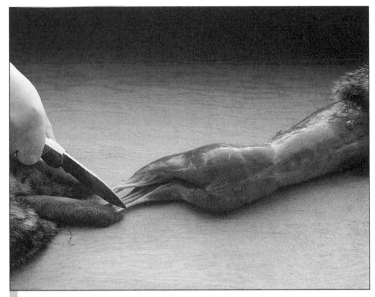

3. CUT off the head, feet, and tail. If you did not field-dress the rabbit before skinning, slit the underside from vent to neck, then remove all internal organs. Save liver and heart if desired.

4. CLEAN body cavity, removing any material left after dressing. Rinse briefly under running water and pat dry.

HOW TO SKIN A SQUIRREL

1. CUT through the base of the tailbone, starting on the underside of the tail. Stop when the bone is severed; do not cut the skin on the top side of the tail.

2. PLACE the squirrel on the ground, and set your foot on the base of the tail. Pull up on the rear legs, peeling the skin all the way to the front legs.

3. PEEL the "britches" off the rear legs to the ankle joints. Keep your foot firmly on the base of the tail until all skinning is complete.

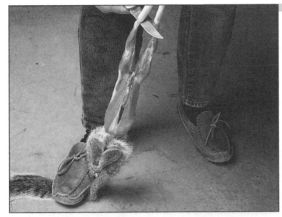

4. REMOVE the squirrel's back feet by cutting through the ankle joints with a knife or game shears. If using a knife, cut away from yourself as pictured.

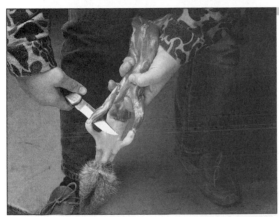

5. PULL each front leg out of the skin, as far as the wrist joint. Use the fingers of your free hand to help loosen the skin at the elbow. Then cut each front foot off at the wrist joint (pictured).

6. CUT the head off. Remove any glands and clean out the body cavity as described in the rabbit-skinning sequence on pages 44-45. Long hairs usually remain on the wrists; cut these off with your knife or shears.

Portioning Small Game

Small game is usually cut into serving pieces before it is cooked or frozen. Pieces are more convenient to freeze than a whole carcass, because they can be arranged into a compact bundle with few air spaces.

The portioning method shown below works with squirrels, rabbits, and hares. Game shears are an excellent tool for this. The rear legs are the meatiest pieces, followed by the saddle or loin portion, then the front legs. The ribs contain very little meat, but can be used for making stock. Remember to wear rubber gloves when handling raw rabbit or hare.

HOW TO CUT UP SMALL GAME *(pictured: Rabbit)*

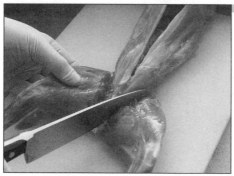

1. PLACE the animal on its back on a cutting board. Cut into the rear leg at a point near the backbone. When you come to the leg bone, stop cutting. If using a game shears, snip the meat around the bone.

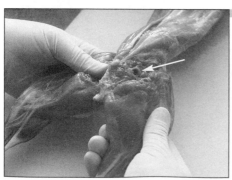

2. BEND the leg back to pop the ball-and-socket joint (arrow). Cut through the joint to remove the leg. Repeat with the other leg. On a large rabbit or hare, each rear leg can be split in two at the knee.

3. REMOVE the front legs by cutting close to the rib cage and behind the shoulder blades. The legs come off easier this way because you don't cut through joints. On a large animal, cut each leg in two at the elbow.

4. CUT the back into two or three pieces, depending on the animal's size. Remove the rib cage, if desired. When portioning a large hare, you can also split the back along the spine, making four to six pieces.

A SIMPLE METHOD FOR CUTTING UP A SQUIRREL

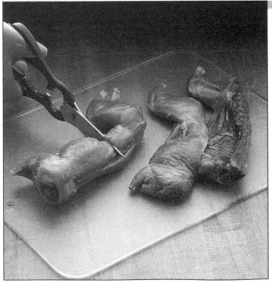

CUT the squirrel in half behind the ribs (left), or along the backbone (right). If the squirrel is small, no further cutting will be necessary. Quarter a large squirrel by cutting each half apart. Quartered squirrels are easier to fry than halved ones and look more attractive when served.

Dressing Upland Birds & Waterfowl

In warm weather, all birds should be gutted as soon as they're shot. In cool weather, gutting can wait until the end of the day's hunt.

Plucking the birds is seldom practical in the middle of a hunt. But if you do have the opportunity, you'll find the feathers pull out more easily then, while the birds are still warm. When plucking in the field, put the feathers in a bag instead of scattering them around. Be sure to check state laws on the transport of game birds. In many states, at least one wing must remain fully feathered and attached to the carcass.

When hunting in warm weather, keep a cooler filled with ice in your car or duck boat. Chill the dressed birds as soon as possible.

Before plucking or skinning any waterfowl, try to determine its age. Old birds may be tough unless cooked with moist heat. Young geese and ducks are smaller than old ones, and the plumage may not be fully colored. If you notice a lot of pinfeathers when plucking, the bird is probably young.

Most upland birds have short life spans, but turkeys and pheasants often live several years. Check the spurs on the legs of a tom turkey or rooster pheasant. Long, pointed spurs indicate an old bird; short, rounded spurs, a young one.

Birds, like big game, can be tenderized by aging. Dress the birds but leave the skin and feathers on; then store them, uncovered, in a refrigerator for a few days.

If possible, birds to be served whole should be plucked rather than skinned. The skin helps keep the meat moist. Waterfowl have thick, tough skin that doesn't tear easily, so they're easier to pluck than upland birds. An upland bird that's badly shot up may have to be skinned, because the delicate skin would rip during plucking. Sage grouse, sea ducks, and fish-eating ducks like mergansers are usually skinned, because the skin of these birds is strongly flavored.

Skinning a bird saves time, although the meat may dry out in cooking. You can save even more time by using the breasting method shown on page 57, if you like pieces instead of a whole bird.

In rare instances, ducks have parasites in the breast meat, which show up as white, rice-like grains. Although safe to eat if thoroughly cooked, the meat is usually unappealing.

HOW TO FIELD-DRESS BIRDS (pictured: Pheasant)

1. CUT the skin from the vent toward the breast-bone using a small hunting knife. Some hunters pluck the feathers between the vent and breastbone before cutting.

2. MAKE a short slit above the breast toward the chin. Pull out the windpipe. Remove the crop, a flexible sac that lies between the bird's breast and chin, and any undigested food it may contain.

3. REMOVE the entrails, including the lungs. If desired, save the heart, gizzard, and liver, storing them in a plastic bag. Be sure to trim the green gall sac from the liver. Wipe the inside of the bird with paper towels.

HOW TO WET-PLUCK A BIRD (pictured: Chukar Partridge)

1. WET the bird thoroughly by holding it underneath a running faucet. If wet-plucking waterfowl, rub the breast with your thumb to ensure that the thick down feathers are saturated with water. Dip the bird several times in simmering (160° to 180°F) water. For waterfowl, add a tablespoon of dishwashing liquid to help saturate the feathers. Rinse any soapy water from the cavity of a field-dressed bird.

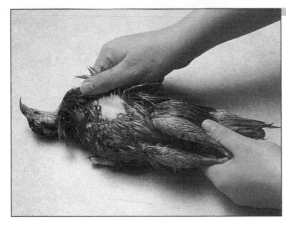

2. RUB the body feathers with your thumb. They should strip off easily. If they don't, dip the bird in hot water again. Pull out the large feathers of the wing and tail, using a pliers if necessary.

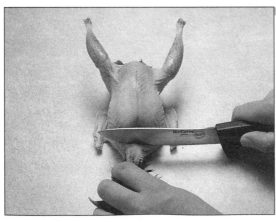

3. CUT off the head and tail. Slice off the feet, removing the leg tendons from upland birds (page 58) if desired. Clean the body cavity and take out the windpipe if still present. Rinse the cavity, and pat the bird dry.

HOW TO WAX WATERFOWL (pictured: Mallard)

1. HEAT a large pot of water to a gentle boil. Melt several chunks of special duck-picking wax or paraffin in the water. The floating layer of melted wax should be at least ¼ inch thick.

2. ROUGH-PLUCK the larger feathers from the body, legs, wings, and tail. Pull only a few feathers at a time. Leave the smaller feathers on the bird, since they make the wax adhere better.

3. DIP the bird in the wax and water. Swish it around gently, then slowly remove it from the wax. Hold the bird up until the wax hardens enough that you can set it down on newspapers without it sticking. Or, hang it by wedging the head between closely spaced nails on a board.

HOW TO WAX WATERFOWL *(continued)*

4. ALLOW the bird to cool until the wax is fairly hard. To speed the process, you can dip the bird in a bucket of cold water. Repeat the dipping and cooling until a layer of wax has built up at least 1/8 inch thick. Allow the wax to cool completely and harden.

5. PEEL the hardened wax off the bird. The feathers will come off with the wax, leaving the skin smooth. You can reuse the wax if you melt it again and strain it through cheesecloth to remove the feathers.

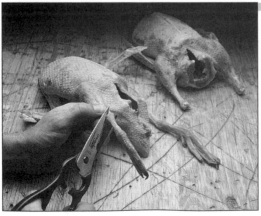

6. CUT off the head, feet, and tail. Remove the windpipe and entrails if the bird was not dressed before waxing. Remove wax from the cavity of a dressed bird. Clean the cavity thoroughly, rinse the bird, and pat it dry.

HOW TO SKIN A BIRD *(pictured: Pheasant)*

1. CUT off the last two joints of the wing with game shears or a knife. Cut off the feet, removing the leg tendons from an upland bird (page 58) if desired.

2. PLACE fingers in the slit where the crop was removed during field-dressing; pull to skin breast and legs. If crop is still in, slit skin and remove crop first.

HOW TO SKIN A BIRD (continued)

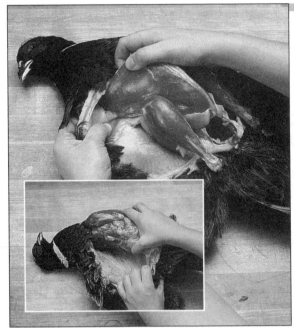

3. PULL the skin away from the wing joints, turning the skin inside-out over the joints as though peeling off a stocking. Free both wings, then peel the skin off the back of the bird (inset).

4. REMOVE the head and tail with game shears. If the bird wasn't dressed before skinning, pull out the windpipe and entrails. Clean the cavity thoroughly. Rinse the bird and pat it dry.

HOW TO BREAST A BIRD TO RETAIN THE LEGS (pictured: Pheasant)

1. CUT off the feet and pull the skin off the breast and legs as described in the skinning sequence on opposite page. Do not skin the wings.

2. SLICE breast halves away from the breastbone, using a fillet knife. Keep the blade as close to the bone as possible. Cut the meat away from the wishbone to free completely.

3. PUSH the leg down, popping the ball-and-socket joint (arrow). Cut through the joint to remove the leg. Remove other leg. If the bird wasn't field-dressed, remove liver, heart, and gizzard if you wish to save them.

4. CUT apart the thigh and drumstick if desired. Dispose of the carcass. With this method of breasting, the only meat discarded is on the back and wings. The boneless breast halves are easy to cook.

HOW TO REMOVE LEG TENDONS FROM UPLAND BIRDS

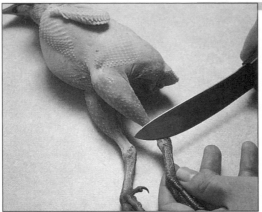

1. CUT the skin around the bottom of the drumstick, either before or after plucking. Do not cut deeply, or you will sever the tendons.

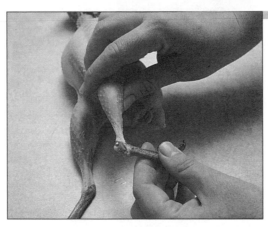

2. BEND the foot back and forth four or five times. This helps loosen the tendons, which connect the foot to the muscles in the leg.

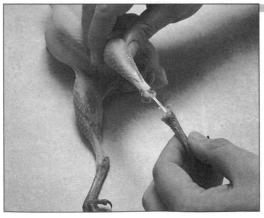

3. PULL the foot off while holding the leg with your other hand. The legs are easier to eat if the tough tendons have been removed.

TIPS FOR DRESSING UPLAND BIRDS AND WATERFOWL

MAKE a large cut when field-dressing a turkey (pictured) or large sage grouse so you can get your whole hand inside the body cavity. This makes it easier to take out the entrails.

REMOVE entrails with a special bird-gutting knife. Insert the hook into the body, then rotate the knife and pull it out. The entrails will twist around the hook. A small forked stick can be used the same way.

SINGE any downy feathers or "hair" with a gas burner. Finish cleaning as described in the last step of the wet-plucking sequence shown on page 52.

BONE the thigh of a pheasant (pictured) or other bird to make a boneless fillet. Fold the thigh in half so the bone is on top. Slip your knife or shears under the end of the bone, and cut the meat away.

Portioning Upland Birds & Waterfowl

Whether to portion a bird, and how, depends mainly on its size and the cooking method. Any upland bird or waterfowl can be cooked whole. The larger ones, such as pheasant, turkey, mallard, and goose, can be cut into traditional pieces if preferred. Birds up to the size of a pheasant can also be split into halves.

If you portion a bird, skinning is optional. When you cut it up, save the backbone, neck, and any bones left from breasting. These parts make excellent stock. Most cooks do not make stock from small birds like doves, woodcock, and quail.

Breasting is quick and easy, and many hunters prefer it when they have a number of birds to process. The breasting method shown on page 57 saves not only the breast but also the thighs and drumsticks, so very little meat is wasted.

HOW TO SPLIT A BIRD INTO HALVES (pictured: Hungarian Partridge)

1. SPLIT the back by cutting along one side of the backbone with game shears. If desired, cut along the other side of the backbone and remove it.

2. CUT along one side of the breastbone and through the wishbone. You can remove the breastbone by making a second cut along the other side of it.

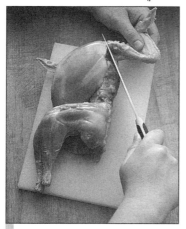

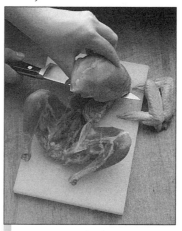

1. REMOVE the wings by cutting through the joint next to the breast.

2. SEPARATE the breast from the back by cutting through the ribs. When you reach the shoulder, grasp the breast in one hand and the back in the other; bend the carcass as if it were hinged. Cut the breast and back apart.

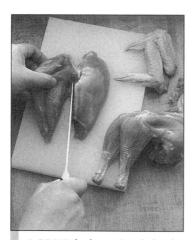

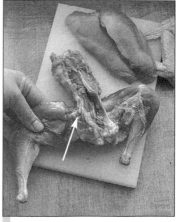

3. DIVIDE the breast into halves by cutting along one side of the breastbone, then cutting away the wishbone. You can also cut along the other side of the breastbone and remove it. Or, bone the breast as shown in the breasting sequence on page 57.

4. BEGIN cutting the leg away from the backbone, then bend it back to expose the ball-and-socket joint (arrow). Cut through the socket to remove the leg. If desired, separate the thigh from the drumstick by cutting through the knee joint.

Birds & Small Game: Final Cleaning Steps

A quick rinse before cooking or freezing is often all that is necessary for the final cleaning step. But a little extra effort will often improve the quality of your meat.

Examine birds and small game carefully, looking for shot and for any fur or feathers the shot may have driven in. Pick all these out with fine tweezers, the point of a sharp knife, or a fly-tying forceps.

Soak the meat only if it is badly shot up and saturated with blood. If so, immerse it for an hour or two in milk, or in a solution of 2 quarts water to 1 tablespoon baking soda. If the meat has been cut into portions, soak only the damaged ones. Rinse the meat well after soaking.

Rinse the hearts and livers to remove any clotted blood. If the top of the heart is ragged, trim it off. The bile sac should have been removed from the liver during field-dressing. Cut away any part of the liver or meat that has a green bile stain.

Some hunters save turkey gizzards, and a few save pheasant and waterfowl gizzards. Clean them as shown in the photo sequence on the opposite page. Gizzards can be fried whole, chopped and mixed into stuffing, or added to the stockpot.

QUICK TIP: Hold a piece of upland bird or small game up to a light. The meat is somewhat transluscent, so you may be able to see shot embedded in it.

1. SPLIT the gizzard between the two lobes, and clean out all food matter and grit. Do not put the contents down a kitchen garbage disposal, since they include small rocks that cannot be ground up.

2. SET the opened gizzard on your cutting board, with the tough inside membrane facing down. Skin the meat from the membrane with a fillet knife. Discard this membrane. The outside membrane can be left on, if desired.

Freezing
Wild Game

Many hunters spend hours dressing and portioning their game, then hurriedly wrap it in a plastic bag and toss it in the freezer. When they defrost it, they're surprised to find their efforts were wasted, because the meat is dried out, or freezer burned.

To prevent freezer burn, double-wrap the meat or freeze it in water. This step is especially important if you own a modern frost-free freezer. In a freezer of this type, a fan unit pulls the moisture out of the air to prevent frost build-up. Unfortunately, it also pulls the moisture out of poorly wrapped meat.

Remove all fat from big game before wrapping it for the freezer. The fat of these animals may turn rancid even while frozen, affecting the taste of the meat.

Backstraps, sirloin tips, and other choice boneless cuts of big game should not be steaked before freezing. Moisture escapes from each cut surface, so smaller pieces lose more moisture than bigger ones. Freeze the whole cut, or divide it into two or three pieces large enough for a family meal. This way, you can use a piece as a roast, or steak it after thawing.

The same principle applies to freezing stew, burger, or sausage meat. Freeze larger chunks, then cut them to size or grind them just before cooking. Game ground with fat for burger meat does not keep as long as plain ground meat, because the fat can turn rancid.

Mark all packages clearly with waterproof, permanent ink. Note the species of animal, the type of cut if applicable, the weight or number of servings, and the date. An old, potentially tough animal should be indicated as such. Some hunters mark with a different color of ink each season, so they can tell at a glance which packages are oldest.

To promote rapid freezing, arrange the wrapped packages in a single layer in the freezer, then turn the freezer to the coldest setting. Stack the packages only after they're frozen.

Thaw frozen game by placing the wrapped package on a plate in the refrigerator at least a full day before you want to cook the meat. The cool temperature minimizes bacterial growth, and the slow thaw helps tenderize the meat.

FREEZER STORAGE CHART

TYPE OF MEAT	WRAPPING METHOD*	MAXIMUM STORAGE TIME
Big-game Roasts	Standard butcher wrap	10 months
Big-game Steaks	Standard butcher wrap	8 months
Big-game Ribs	Foil wrap	5 months
Big-game Organs	Standard butcher wrap	4 months
	Water pack	6 months
Big-game Chunks	Freezer bag and paper	6 months
Big-game Burger	Freezer bag and paper	4 months
Cut-up Small Game	Standard butcher wrap	8 months
	Water pack	1 year
Small-game Organs	Water pack	10 months
Whole Large Birds	Foil wrap	5 months
Whole Small Birds	Standard butcher wrap	6 months
	Water pack	1 year
Cut-up Upland Birds	Standard butcher wrap	8 months
	Water pack	1 year
Cut-up Waterfowl	Standard butcher wrap	8 months
	Water pack	1 year
Bird Giblets	Water pack	4 months
Game Stock	Freezer containers	4 months

Photo instructions given for all wrapping techniques on pages 66-73.

THE STANDARD BUTCHER WRAP

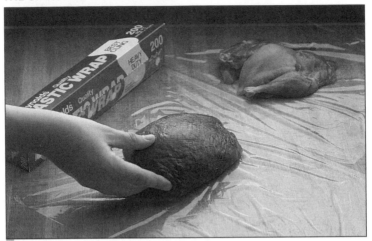

1. PLACE the meat on the center of a large piece of plastic wrap. If wrapping a cut-up bird or small-game animal, arrange the pieces to form a compact bundle, with as little space between them as possible. For ribs or other odd-shaped cuts, use heavy-duty aluminum foil in place of plastic wrap.

2. BRING one end of the wrap over the meat, then fold both sides over it. Gently squeeze out as much air as possible. Bring the other end over, or roll the bundle to it, continuing to squeeze out air.

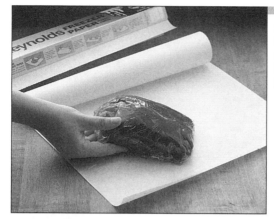

3. LAY the wrapped bundle on a corner of a large piece of heavy-duty freezer paper (shiny side up).

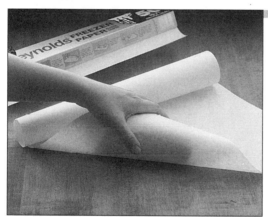

4. ROLL the bundle once, so both the top and bottom are covered with a single layer of freezer paper.

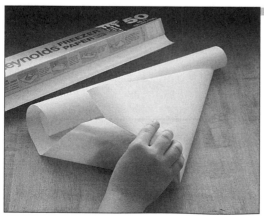

5. FOLD one side of the freezer paper over the bundle. Tuck in any loose edges of the paper.

THE STANDARD BUTCHER WRAP (continued)

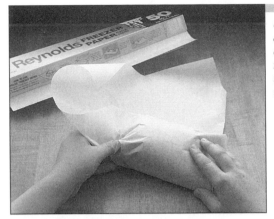

6. ROLL the bundle again. Fold the other side of the freezer paper over the bundle, tucking the corner neatly.

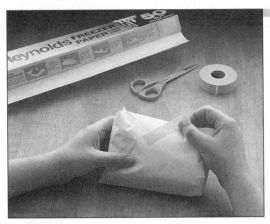

7. FASTEN the end with freezer tape when wrapping is complete. Tape the seam also, if desired.

8. LABEL with a waterproof pen. Note the species, cut, quantity, date, and maturity of animal if relevant.

HOW TO WRAP A WHOLE LARGE GAME BIRD

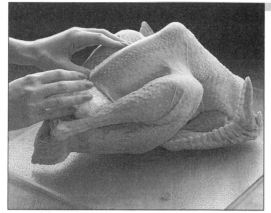

1. STUFF wadded plastic wrap into the body cavity. This reduces the chance of freezer burn.

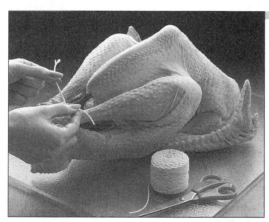

2. TIE the drumsticks together with kitchen string. They'll stick out less, and wrapping will be easier.

3. WRAP the bird with heavy-duty aluminum foil. You may need several pieces to cover the entire bird. Press the foil snugly around the body. Complete the wrapping with a double layer of heavy-duty freezer paper. Seal all the seams with freezer tape, and label the package.

HOW TO WATER-PACK GAME IN CONTAINERS

1. PLACE game in clean, waxed dairy cartons or plastic containers. Use pint- or quart-sized cartons for small whole birds, half-gallon cartons for large ones. Tiny birds like woodcock or doves can be frozen four to six per carton. Layer giblets in a small carton. Arrange cut-up birds or small game in a plastic container. Cover the game with water, jiggle it to eliminate air bubbles, and freeze.

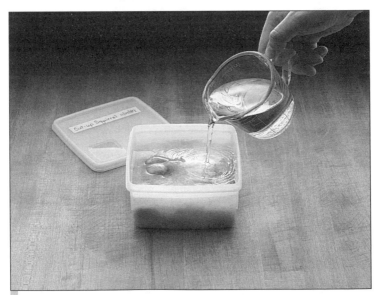

2. CHECK after the water is frozen to be sure the game is completely covered with a layer of ice. If not, add cold water and refreeze.

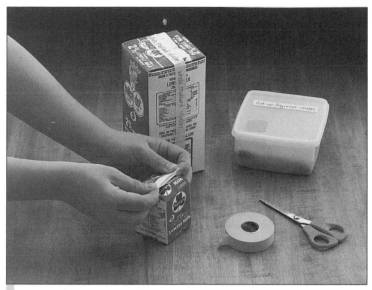

3. FOLD the top of a dairy carton closed, if possible. Wrap a band of freezer tape around the carton so it sticks to itself. Label the container.

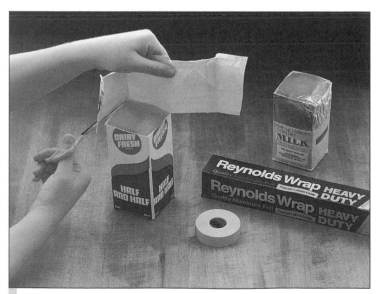

4. CUT off the top if the carton can't be closed, or if it isn't filled to the fold with ice. Trim at the ice level. Cover the top with heavy-duty aluminum foil. Wrap freezer tape around the edge of the foil, and label it.

HOW TO WATER-PACK CUT-UP GAME IN A PLASTIC BAG

1. LAY a zippered plastic freezer bag in a cake pan, then arrange the pieces in the bag.

2. ADD water to completely cover the pieces of game. Squeeze out all the air, and seal the top of the bag. Set the pan in the freezer.

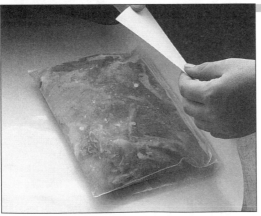

3. BUTCHER-WRAP the frozen bag with freezer paper. This keeps it from ripping or puncturing, which could expose the meat to freezer burn.

TIPS FOR FREEZING GAME

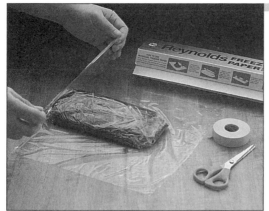

TRIPLE-WRAP cut steaks or chops for additional protection from freezer burn. Use two layers of plastic wrap, then finish with a layer of freezer paper.

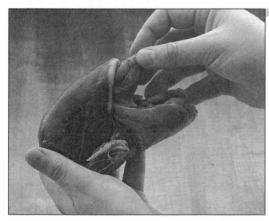

TUCK the legs of a partridge, quail, or other small bird into the body cavity before wrapping. The package will be more compact, with less air inside to dry the meat.

PUT stew chunks or ground meat in a zippered plastic freezer bag. To push out air, immerse the bag almost to its top in a sinkful of cold water. Seal the bag while it's still in the water. Wrap it in freezer paper.

2

BIG GAME:
RECIPES

Cooking Big Game

Big-game meat, if cooked properly, is even tastier than choice beef. And because it's leaner than beef, it also has fewer calories. But the lean meat can become tough and dry if cooked incorrectly.

To make sure big-game meat doesn't dry out, cook it with moist heat or keep it on the rare side. The only exceptions are the meat of bears and wild pigs. Always cook these meats thoroughly, like pork, because they may carry the parasite that causes trichinosis.

The external fat of big game is strong tasting and tallowy, so remove it before cooking. To tenderize tough cuts, marinate them in a mixture of oil and wine or in a packaged beef marinade.

Most recipes for deer work equally well for antelope, elk, and moose. Generally, antelope and elk meat is finer-grained than deer and moose meat. Of the antlered animals, elk probably tastes most like beef; antelope, least like it. Bear meat is stronger, darker, and coarser than other big game and is usually prepared with more seasoning.

How good the meat tastes, however, depends less on the species of animal than on its sex and age, the time of year it was killed, and the care you take with it after the kill. A buck taken during the rut, for instance, is usually stronger tasting and tougher than one taken earlier in the season.

The animal's diet also affects the flavor. A corn-fed deer is much tastier than one forced to eat low-nutrition foods like red cedar. If you store meat from several animals in your freezer and notice that meat from one tastes particularly strong, mark all the other packages from that animal. Then you can prepare this meat in a way that minimizes the flavor.

SUBSTITUTION GUIDE

Although there are differences in flavor, texture, and fat content among the meats from the various hoofed big-game species, you can successfully substitute them for deer in a recipe, keeping in mind the tenderness of the specified cut and that of the substitute.

The substitution chart below shows the various big-game cuts you can substitute for the most common deer cuts. In addition, suggested cooking methods help you make the most of specific cuts.

SUBSTITUTION CHART

DEER CUT	TENDERNESS	SUBSTITUTE	COOKING METHOD
Tenderloin (whole)	Very tender	Tenderloin portion from moose, elk or caribou; Loin portion from caribou, deer or antelope	Oven roast, grill
Loin (portion)	Tender	Loin portion from moose, elk or caribou; Tenderloin (whole) from moose, elk or caribou	Oven roast, broil, grill, pan-broil, panfry
Loin steak	Tender	Loin steak from moose, elk or caribou; Tenderloin from moose, elk, caribou, deer or antelope	Broil, grill, panbroil, panfry
Loin chop	Tender	Loin chop from any big-game animal	Broil, grill, pan-broil, panfry
Rump roast	Intermediate tender	Rump roast from any big-game animal; Deer sirloin tip; Rolled, tied bottom round from deer or antelope; Eye of round from moose, elk or caribou	Oven roast, broil, grill, pan-broil, panfry
Round steak	Intermediate tender	Round steak from any big-game animal; Sirloin steak from any big-game animal; Loin chop from moose, elk, caribou, deer or antelope	Broil, grill, pan-broil, panfry, stir-fry (strips)
Boneless rolled shoulder roast	Less tender	Boneless rolled shoulder roast from any big-game animal; Rolled rib roast from moose, elk or caribou; Boneless chuck roast from moose, elk or caribou	Braise
Bone-in chuck roast	Less tender	Bone-in chuck roast from any big-game animal; Blade pot roast from moose, elk or caribou	Braise

TIPS FOR PREPARING BIG-GAME MEAT

REMOVE silverskin with a fillet knife. Cut into one end of the meat to the silverskin. Turn blade parallel to silverskin. Hold silverskin firmly with fingertips, and push knife away from them as though skinning a fish fillet. Very little meat is removed with the silverskin this way.

BUTTERFLY small-diameter backstraps or tenderloins to make larger steaks. Cut a steak twice as thick as you want. Then slice it into two "wings" of equal thickness; leave the two wings joined by an edge of meat. Open steak up, and flatten slightly.

CUT across the grain of the meat when steaking it or making slices for sautéeing. Cut with the grain, however, when making slices for jerky. Partially frozen meat is easiest to slice.

CHOP or grind trimmed big-game scrap with 15 to 20% beef fat to make burger. Use a food processor or meat grinder with sharp blades. Fat is easiest to chop if kept very cold.

ROASTING BIG GAME

There are two basic ways to roast big game: with dry heat and moist heat. Dry-heat roasting includes high- and low-temperature methods. The most common method of moist-heat roasting is braising, which includes pot roasting.

Only prime roasts are candidates for dry-heat, high-temperature cooking. These include the top round, sirloin tip, backstrap, and rump roasts. The tenderloin of a moose, elk or large deer may also be used. These prime cuts are naturally tender and do not need long, slow cooking for tenderizing.

For high-temperature cooking, select a roast between 2 and 5 inches thick, or a thinner piece you can roll and tie (pages 40-41). First, brown the meat in hot fat, then roast it in a hot (400° to 450°F) oven. With these high temperatures, roasts should be cooked only rare to medium. If cooked well done, they dry out and shrink.

Low-temperature roasting is another option for these same prime cuts. And it's necessary for such medium-tender cuts as the bottom round and eye of round, which need longer cooking to ensure tenderness. Cover the meat with bacon or a sheet of beef or pork fat (available from your butcher), or baste it frequently. Cook it in a slow (300° to 325°F) oven. With low heat, roasts may be cooked rare, medium or well done.

When roasting with dry heat, use a meat thermometer to check for doneness. The chart below gives temperatures for various stages of doneness. Remove the meat from the oven when it reads 5° below the ideal temperature; it will continue to cook on the platter. It will slice better if you wait 10 to 15 minutes before carving.

Moist heat tenderizes shoulder roasts and other tough cuts, and also works well with the bottom round and eye of round. Brown the roast in hot fat, then add liquid and seasonings and cover the pan tightly. Cook the meat until tender, in a moderate (325° to 350°F) oven. When pot roasting, add vegetables during the last hour or so of cooking. Braised meat is always served well done.

INTERNAL TEMPERATURE DONENESS CHART

DONENESS	INTERNAL TEMPERATURE
Rare	130° to 135°F
Medium-rare	135° to 140°F
Medium	140° to 145°F
Medium-well	150° to 155°F
Well done	155° to 160°F

Big-Game Recipes

ROAST BONELESS SIRLOIN TIP

1 boneless deer or antelope sirloin tip roast or other suitable
   roast, 2 to 5 inches thick
1 to 2 tablespoons olive oil or vegetable oil

2 to 4 servings per pound

Heat oven to 450°. In medium skillet or Dutch oven, sear
roast well on all sides in oil over medium-high heat. Place
on rack in roasting pan. Roast to desired doneness (see
chart on opposite page), 18 to 28 minutes per pound;
remove roast when temperature is 5° less than desired.
Allow meat to rest for 10 to 15 minutes before carving.

ROAST BIG-GAME TENDERLOIN

1 whole elk, moose, or large deer tenderloin, 1½ to 3½ pounds
   Peanut or vegetable oil
   Salt and freshly ground black pepper
1 recipe Madeira Game Sauce (page 177), optional

2 to 4 servings per pound

Heat oven to 450°. Place tenderloin in roasting pan; tuck
small end under. Brush tenderloin with oil. Roast at 450° for
10 minutes. Reduce heat to 350°. Roast to desired doneness
(see chart on opposite page), 20 to 25 minutes per pound;
remove roast when temperature is 5° less than desired. Allow
meat to rest for 10 minutes before carving. Sprinkle with salt
and pepper. Serve with Madeira Game Sauce, if desired.

81

PEPPERED ANTELOPE ROAST ↑

2 medium cloves garlic
1 boneless rolled antelope or deer top round roast or other
   suitable roast, 3 to 5 pounds
   Vegetable oil
   Cracked black pepper
8 to 10 slices bacon

2 to 4 servings per pound

Heat oven to 325°. Cut each garlic clove into 4 or 5 slivers. Make 8 or 10 shallow slits in roast. Insert a garlic sliver into each slit. Place roast on rack in roasting pan; brush with oil. Sprinkle pepper liberally over roast. Cover roast with bacon slices. Roast to desired doneness (see chart on page 80), 22 to 32 minutes per pound; remove roast when temperature is 5° less than desired. Allow meat to rest for 10 to 15 minutes before carving. Serve with pan juices.

BIG-GAME POT ROAST

¹/₃ cup all-purpose flour
1 teaspoon dried basil leaves
¹/₂ teaspoon dried marjoram
    leaves
¹/₂ teaspoon dried thyme leaves
¹/₂ teaspoon salt
¹/₄ teaspoon pepper
2¹/₂- to 3-pound deer, antelope,
    elk, moose, or bear roast
3 tablespoons vegetable oil

1 can (10¹/₂ ounces) condensed
    French onion soup
¹/₂ cup water, broth, or wine
1 bay leaf
1 rutabaga, peeled and cut
    into 1-inch cubes
4 to 6 medium carrots, cut
    into 2-inch pieces
3 stalks celery, cut into
    2-inch pieces

4 to 6 servings

Heat oven to 350°. In large plastic food-storage bag, combine flour, basil, marjoram, thyme, salt, and pepper; shake
to mix. Add meat; shake to coat. In Dutch oven, brown
meat on both sides in oil. Add remaining flour mixture,
soup, water, and bay leaf. Heat to boiling. Remove from
heat; cover. Bake for 1¹/₂ hours. Add rutabaga, carrots, and
celery. Recover. Bake until meat and vegetables are tender,
1 to 1¹/₂ hours longer. Discard bay leaf before serving.

ROLLED STUFFED ROAST OF VENISON →

6 slices bacon
1 medium onion, chopped
1/2 cup chopped celery
1/2 cup chopped carrot
1/3 cup seasoned dry bread crumbs
2 teaspoons dried parsley flakes
1/4 teaspoon salt
1/8 teaspoon pepper
3- to 4-pound boneless deer, antelope, elk, or moose roast, up
    to 1 inch thick
3 slices bacon, cut in half

6 to 8 servings

Heat oven to 325°. Fry 6 slices bacon in large skillet over medium heat until crisp. Remove from heat. Transfer bacon to paper towels to drain. Reserve 3 tablespoons bacon fat. Crumble drained bacon; set aside.

Sauté onion, celery, and carrot in reserved bacon fat over medium heat until tender. Remove from heat. Stir in crumbled bacon, bread crumbs, parsley flakes, salt, and pepper. Spread vegetable mixture evenly on roast and pat firmly into place. Roll up jelly-roll style, rolling with the grain of the meat. Tie roast with kitchen string (pages 40-41). Place in roasting pan. Top roast with 3 halved slices bacon. Roast to desired doneness (see chart on page 80), 22 to 30 minutes per pound.

VENISON ROAST BURGUNDY LOW-FAT

2 tablespoons all-purpose flour
1 cup burgundy
1/2 teaspoon dried rosemary
1/2 teaspoon dried marjoram
1/2 teaspoon salt
1/4 teaspoon pepper
3- to 4-pound deer, elk, or
    moose roast

4 carrots, cut into 2-inch
    pieces
2 medium onions, quartered
2 bay leaves
1 tablespoon cornstarch
1/4 cup cold water
1/2 teaspoon brown bouquet
    sauce, optional

6 to 8 servings

Heat oven to 350°. Add flour to large (14 × 20-inch) oven cooking bag; shake to distribute. Place bag in roasting pan. Pour wine into bag; stir with plastic or wooden spoon to blend into flour. Set aside.

In small mixing bowl, mix rosemary, marjoram, salt, and pepper. Rub mixture evenly over meat. Place meat in cooking bag. Add carrots, onions, and bay leaves to bag and close with provided nylon tie. Make six 1/2-inch slits in top of bag. Roast until meat is tender, 1 1/2 to 2 1/2 hours. Remove meat to heated platter. With slotted spoon, transfer vegetables to platter. Keep warm. Discard bay leaves. Pour juices into small saucepan. In 1-cup measure, blend cornstarch into water. Stir half of cornstarch mixture into juices. Heat to boiling, stirring constantly. Cook, stirring constantly, until thickened and bubbly. Blend in additional cornstarch if thicker gravy is desired; cook and stir until thickened and bubbly. Stir in bouquet sauce. Serve gravy with meat and vegetables.

BIG GAME BELGIUM

1/2 cup all-purpose flour
2 teaspoons dried thyme leaves
1/4 teaspoon salt
1/2 teaspoon pepper
3- pound elk shoulder roast, about 2 inches thick
3 tablespoons olive oil or vegetable oil
1/2 pound salt pork, diced
3 tablespoons butter or margarine
3 medium onions, thinly sliced
1 tablespoon granulated sugar
1 bottle (12 ounces) dark beer
2 tablespoons packed brown sugar
1 tablespoon snipped fresh parsley

4 to 6 servings

Heat oven to 325°. In large plastic food-storage bag, combine flour, thyme, salt, and pepper; shake to mix. Add meat; shake to coat. In Dutch oven, brown meat in oil over medium heat. Remove meat; set aside. Add salt pork to Dutch oven. Cook over medium heat, stirring frequently, until salt pork is crisp and golden brown. With slotted spoon, transfer salt pork to small mixing bowl; set aside. Melt butter in Dutch oven. Add onions. Cook and stir over medium heat until tender. Add granulated sugar. Cook and stir until onions are brown, about 10 minutes. Add beer and brown sugar. Stir, scraping bottom of pan to loosen browned bits. Return meat to Dutch oven. Add reserved salt pork. Cover; bake until meat is tender, about 2 hours. Transfer meat to platter. Garnish with parsley. Serve with pan juices and buttered noodles if desired.

FILLET OF VENISON LOW-FAT VERY FAST

1 whole deer tenderloin, 1 to 3 pounds
1 to 2 tablespoons butter or margarine
1 tablespoon olive oil or vegetable oil
   Salt and freshly ground black pepper
   Madeira Game Sauce (page 177), optional

2 or 3 servings per pound

Remove all surface fat and silverskin from tenderloin. Slice across grain into 1-inch-thick fillets. In medium skillet, melt butter in oil over medium-low heat. Add fillets; cook to desired doneness over medium-high heat, turning once. Salt and pepper to taste. Serve with Madeira Game Sauce.

BIG-GAME BAKED ROUND STEAK

2 to 3 pounds boneless deer, antelope, elk, or moose round steak, 1 inch thick
1/2 cup all-purpose flour
2 teaspoons salt
1/4 teaspoon pepper
1 to 2 tablespoons butter or margarine
2 to 3 tablespoons olive oil or vegetable oil

3 tablespoons finely chopped onion
Brown sugar
Catsup
Dried basil leaves
1 tablespoon butter or margarine, cut up
1/4 cup venison stock (page 175) or beef broth

6 to 8 servings

Heat oven to 350°. Trim meat; cut into serving-sized pieces. Pound to 1/2-inch thickness with meat mallet. On a sheet of waxed paper, mix flour, salt, and pepper. Dip steaks in flour mixture, turning to coat. In large skillet, melt 1 tablespoon butter in 2 tablespoons oil over medium-high heat. Add coated steaks; brown on both sides. Fry in two batches if necessary, adding additional butter and oil. Arrange browned steaks in 12 × 8-inch baking pan. Sprinkle with onion. Top each steak with 1 teaspoon packed brown sugar and 1 teaspoon catsup. Sprinkle lightly with basil. Dot with 1 tablespoon butter. Add stock to drippings in skillet. Cook over medium heat for about 1 minute, stirring to loosen any browned bits. Add to baking pan. Cover with aluminum foil. Bake for about 45 minutes. Remove foil. If meat appears dry, add a small amount of stock or water to pan. Bake uncovered until browned on top, about 15 minutes longer.

BIG-GAME SWISS STEAK LOW-FAT

1½ pounds boneless deer round steak or other big-game steak, ½ to 1 inch thick
⅓ cup all-purpose flour
1 teaspoon salt
¼ teaspoon pepper
3 to 4 tablespoons bacon fat
1 can (16 ounces) stewed tomatoes

¾ cup water
1 teaspoon instant beef bouillon granules
½ teaspoon dried basil leaves
½ teaspoon dried marjoram leaves
1 medium onion, thinly sliced

4 to 6 servings

Trim meat; cut into serving-sized pieces. Pound to ¼- to ½-inch thickness with meat mallet. On a sheet of waxed paper, mix flour, salt, and pepper. Dip steaks in flour mixture, turning to coat. In large skillet, heat bacon fat over medium heat. Add coated steaks; brown lightly on both sides. Fry in two batches if necessary. In small mixing bowl, mix stewed tomatoes, water, bouillon granules, basil, and marjoram; pour over steaks. Top meat and tomatoes with sliced onion. Heat to boiling. Reduce heat; cover. Simmer over very low heat until meat is tender, 1½ to 2 hours. Skim fat if desired.

← GRILLED LOIN WITH BROWN SUGAR BASTE

2 to 4 pounds deer, antelope, elk, or
    moose loin portion or whole backstrap
3 tablespoons butter or margarine
3 tablespoons soy sauce
3 tablespoons packed brown sugar

2 or 3 servings per pound

Start charcoal briquets in grill. Remove all fat and silverskin from meat. Cut into lengths about 4 inches long, or about 6 to 8 ounces each. In small saucepan, melt butter over medium heat. Add soy sauce and brown sugar. Cook, stirring constantly, until brown sugar dissolves and sauce bubbles.

When charcoal briquets are covered with ash, spread them evenly in grill. Place grate above hot coals. Place meat on grate. Grill on one side until seared. Turn meat over; brush with brown sugar mixture. Continue grilling, brushing frequently with brown sugar mixture and turning occasionally to grill all sides, until desired doneness.

BEAR STEAK FLAMADE

1/3 cup all-purpose flour
1 teaspoon salt
1/4 teaspoon pepper
2 pounds bear round steak, 1 inch thick
1/2 cup butter or margarine, divided
2 tablespoons olive oil or vegetable oil

4 medium onions, thinly sliced
1 1/2 cups beer
1/4 teaspoon dried marjoram leaves
1/4 teaspoon dried thyme leaves
1 bay leaf

6 to 8 servings

Heat oven to 325°. On a sheet of waxed paper, mix flour, salt, and pepper. Dip steak in flour mixture, turning to coat. In large skillet, melt 1/4 cup butter in oil over medium-low heat. Add steak; brown on both sides over medium-high heat. Transfer meat and drippings to 3-quart casserole; set aside.

In large skillet, melt remaining 1/4 cup butter over medium-low heat. Add onions, stirring to coat with butter. Cover. Cook until tender but not brown, about 10 minutes. Pour onions over steak in casserole. Add remaining ingredients. Cover. Bake until meat is tender, 2 to 2 1/2 hours. Discard bay leaf before serving.

VENISON PICATTA →

1¼ pounds deer, antelope, elk, or
    moose loin
2 cups milk, divided
½ cup all-purpose flour
½ teaspoon salt
½ teaspoon pepper
¼ cup butter or margarine
¾ cup dry white wine
2 to 3 tablespoons fresh lemon
    juice
¼ cup snipped fresh parsley
1 to 2 tablespoons capers,
    drained

3 or 4 servings

Slice loin across the grain into thin slices, ¼ inch thick or
less.* In shallow dish, combine meat and 1 cup milk.
Cover dish with plastic wrap. Refrigerate for 1 to 3 hours.
Drain and discard milk. Add remaining 1 cup milk. Let
stand at room temperature for 1 hour. Drain and discard
milk. Pat venison slices dry with paper towels.

On a sheet of waxed paper, mix flour, salt, and pepper.
Dip venison slices in flour mixture, turning to coat. In
large skillet, melt butter over medium-high heat. Add venison slices; brown on both sides. Add wine; cook about 2
minutes. Transfer venison slices to heated platter with slotted spoon. Add lemon juice, parsley, and capers to skillet.
Reduce heat to medium. Cook, stirring constantly, about 2
minutes, scraping bottom and sides of skillet. Serve sauce
over venison slices.

*TIP: The venison will be easier to slice thinly if partially frozen.

CHICKEN-FRIED VENISON STEAKS

1 to 1½ pounds boneless
deer, antelope, elk, or
moose round steak, about
½ inch thick
⅓ cup milk
1 egg
⅓ cup all-purpose flour
½ teaspoon salt
⅛ teaspoon pepper

2 tablespoons butter or
margarine
2 tablespoons vegetable oil

GRAVY:
1¼ cups milk
2 tablespoons all-purpose flour
¼ teaspoon salt
Dash pepper

3 or 4 servings

Trim meat; cut into serving-sized pieces. Pound to ¼-inch
thickness with meat mallet. In 9-inch pie plate, blend ⅓ cup
milk and the egg. On a sheet of waxed paper, mix ⅓ cup
flour, ½ teaspoon salt, and ⅛ teaspoon pepper. Dip steaks in
milk mixture, then in flour mixture, turning to coat. Set aside.

In large skillet, melt butter in oil over medium-low heat.
Add steaks; brown on both sides over medium-high heat.
Fry in two batches, if necessary. Remove to heated platter.
Set aside and keep warm. In small bowl, blend milk into
remaining gravy ingredients. Blend into pan drippings.
Cook over medium heat, stirring constantly, until thick-
ened and bubbly. Strain if desired. Serve gravy with steaks.

OLD-FASHIONED VENISON STEW LOW-FAT

1½ cups water
½ cup beer
2 envelopes (⅞ ounce each) onion gravy mix
1 tablespoon packed brown sugar
¼ teaspoon ground thyme
2 to 3 pounds deer, antelope, elk, or moose stew meat
3 tablespoons vegetable oil
1 bay leaf
6 carrots, cut into 1-inch pieces
6 medium parsnips, cut into 1-inch cubes
1 cup frozen peas

6 to 8 servings

In small mixing bowl, blend water, beer, gravy mix, brown sugar, and thyme. Set aside. Remove all fat and silverskin from meat. Cut into 1-inch pieces. In Dutch oven, brown meat in oil over medium-high heat. Add beer mixture and bay leaf to Dutch oven. Reduce heat; cover. Simmer until meat is almost tender, 1 to 1½ hours, stirring occasionally. Add carrots and parsnips; re-cover. Cook 20 minutes longer. Add peas; re-cover. Cook 5 to 10 minutes longer. Discard bay leaf before serving.

SPICY ELK KABOBS

MARINADE:

1/4 cup finely chopped onion
1/4 cup white wine
2 tablespoons vegetable oil
2 tablespoons soy sauce
1 tablespoon packed brown sugar
2 teaspoons ground coriander
1 teaspoon chili powder
1/2 teaspoon salt
1/2 teaspoon lemon pepper seasoning
1/8 teaspoon crushed red pepper flakes

1 pound elk steak, cut into
  1-inch cubes
2 cups water
1 medium zucchini (6 to 8 ounces),
  cut into 3/4-inch slices
1 sweet red pepper, cut into 16 pieces

4 servings

In medium saucepan, combine all marinade ingredients. Heat to boiling, stirring occasionally. Cool to room temperature. Add elk cubes. Toss to coat with marinade. Cover; marinate at room temperature for 30 minutes.

While elk is marinating, heat water to boiling in medium saucepan. Add zucchini. Return to boiling. Boil 2 minutes. Drain and rinse under cold water.

With slotted spoon, lift elk cubes from marinade. Set marinade aside. Divide elk, zucchini, and pepper into four groups. For each kabob, alternate elk with zucchini and pepper on 12-inch kabob skewer. Arrange kabobs on broiler pan. Set oven to broil and/or 550°. Broil kabobs 2 to 3 inches from heat until meat is desired doneness, 6 to 12 minutes, turning kabobs and brushing with marinade once.

Variation: Substitute deer, antelope, or moose for the elk.

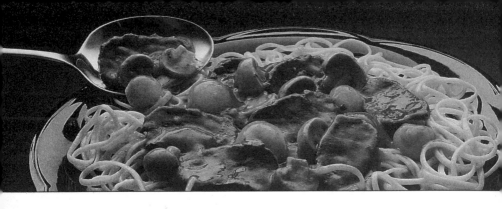

ELK TENDERLOIN SAUTÉ

2 cups water
1 teaspoon salt
1/2 pound fresh pearl onions
  (about 1 1/3 cups)
1/4 cup all-purpose flour
1/2 teaspoon salt
1/4 teaspoon pepper
1 1/2 pounds elk tenderloin,
  thinly sliced
2 tablespoons butter or
  margarine
2 tablespoons vegetable oil
1 3/4 cups venison stock
  (page 175) or beef broth

1 can (16 ounces) whole
  tomatoes, cut up and
  drained
1/2 cup burgundy
1/4 cup tomato paste
1 teaspoon Worcestershire
  sauce
1/4 teaspoon dried thyme
  leaves
1 or 2 cloves garlic, minced
2 bay leaves
1/2 pound fresh mushrooms,
  cut into halves
Hot cooked rice or noodles

4 to 6 servings

In small saucepan, heat water and 1 teaspoon salt to boiling. Add onions. Return to boiling. Reduce heat; cover. Simmer until onions are just tender, about 15 minutes. Drain and rinse under cold water. Set aside.

In large plastic food-storage bag, combine flour, 1/2 teaspoon salt, and the pepper; shake to mix. Add elk slices; shake to coat. In large skillet, melt butter in oil over medium heat. Add elk slices. Cook over medium-high heat until browned but still rare, stirring occasionally. Remove with slotted spoon; set aside. Add remaining ingredients except mushrooms and rice to cooking liquid in skillet; mix well. Add mushrooms and reserved onions. Heat to boiling. Reduce heat; cover. Simmer 10 minutes. Stir in elk slices. Cook, uncovered, over medium-low heat until slightly thickened, about 5 minutes. Discard bay leaves before serving. Serve over rice.

BEAR STEW

1½ to 2 pounds bear stew meat
¼ cup all-purpose flour
1 teaspoon dried marjoram leaves
1 teaspoon salt
⅛ teaspoon pepper
2 tablespoons vegetable oil
1 can (16 ounces) whole tomatoes, undrained
1 cup water
¼ cup white wine or water
1 tablespoon vinegar
1 medium onion, cut in half lengthwise and
    thinly sliced
½ cup chopped celery
2 cloves garlic, minced
1 bay leaf
2 medium baking potatoes

4 to 6 servings

Remove all fat and silverskin from meat. Cut into 1-inch pieces. In large plastic food-storage bag, combine flour, marjoram, salt, and pepper; shake to mix. Add meat; shake to coat. In heavy medium saucepan, heat oil over medium-high heat until hot. Add meat and flour mixture. Brown, stirring occasionally. Add remaining ingredients except potatoes; mix well. Heat to boiling. Reduce heat; cover. Simmer 1 hour, stirring occasionally.

Cut potatoes into 1-inch chunks. Add to saucepan. Heat to boiling. Reduce heat; cover. Simmer until meat and potatoes are tender, about 1 hour, stirring occasionally. Discard bay leaf before serving.

OVEN-BARBECUED VENISON RIBS ◆ LOW-FAT

SAUCE:

1/2 cup catsup
1/2 cup water
·1/4 cup cider vinegar
1/4 cup finely chopped onion
3 tablespoons packed brown sugar
2 tablespoons Worcestershire sauce
1 tablespoon lemon juice
1 tablespoon paprika
1 teaspoon dry mustard
1 teaspoon salt
1 teaspoon liquid smoke flavoring
1/2 teaspoon pepper
1/4 teaspoon chili powder

2 to 3 pounds deer, antelope, elk, or moose ribs
2 cups water

4 servings

In small bowl, combine all sauce ingredients. Mix well. In Dutch oven, combine ribs, 2 cups water, and 3/4 cup sauce, reserving remaining sauce. Heat rib mixture to boiling. Reduce heat; cover. Simmer until ribs are tender, about 1 hour, rearranging ribs once or twice.

Heat oven to 350°. Arrange ribs on roasting pan. Brush with reserved sauce. Bake for 10 minutes. Turn ribs over. Brush with sauce. Bake for 10 minutes longer. Serve with remaining sauce.

ORIENTAL-STYLE GRILLED VENISON RIBS ◆ LOW-FAT

MARINADE:

1 1/2 cups dry sherry
1/4 cup peanut oil or vegetable oil
1/4 cup rice wine vinegar
6 tablespoons soy sauce
6 tablespoons plum sauce or 3 tablespoons plum jelly
2 tablespoons hoisin sauce
1 tablespoon minced fresh gingerroot
4 cloves garlic, minced

2 to 3 pounds deer, antelope, elk, or moose ribs

4 servings

In medium saucepan, combine all marinade ingredients. Heat over medium heat, stirring constantly, until hot. Cool to room temperature. Place ribs in 13 × 9-inch baking pan, or in an oven cooking bag. Pour cooled marinade over ribs. Cover pan with plastic wrap or seal bag. Marinate ribs for 1 to 2 hours, turning ribs several times.

Start charcoal briquets in grill. When briquets are covered with ash, spread them evenly in grill. Place grate above hot coals. Arrange ribs on grate. Grill until cooked through, 10 to 15 minutes, turning once. Serve with remaining sauce.

VENISON VEGETABLE SOUP  ◆LOW-FAT

1½ to 2 pounds deer, antelope, elk, or moose bones, fairly meaty
2 stalks celery, thinly sliced
2 medium carrots, thinly sliced
1 medium onion, finely chopped
2 cloves garlic, minced
2 tablespoons butter or margarine
3 quarts water
1 bay leaf
1 tablespoon salt
¾ teaspoon dried marjoram leaves
1½ to 2 cups cubed cooked deer, antelope, elk, or moose
1 can (16 ounces) stewed tomatoes, undrained
1 package (10 ounces) frozen corn

About 4 quarts

Heat oven to 400°. Arrange bones in a single layer in large roasting pan or on baking sheet. Bake uncovered until bones are browned, 10 to 20 minutes. Drain, if needed. Set bones aside.

In Dutch oven, cook and stir celery, carrots, onion, and garlic in butter over medium heat until tender. Add browned bones, water, bay leaf, salt, and marjoram. Heat to boiling. Reduce heat; cover. Simmer until meat on bones is very tender, 1½ to 2 hours. Remove bones; cool slightly. Remove meat from bones; discard bones. Return meat to Dutch oven. Add remaining ingredients. Simmer, uncovered, 1 hour longer. Discard bay leaf before serving.

ORANGE ONION LIVER *FAST*

1/4 cup all-purpose flour
1/8 teaspoon salt
1/8 teaspoon pepper
 1 pound deer, antelope, elk, or moose liver,
    trimmed and sliced 1/2 inch thick
1/4 cup butter or margarine
 1 medium yellow onion, thinly sliced
 1 medium red onion, thinly sliced
 1 tablespoon sugar
 1 medium orange, sliced
1/4 cup butter or margarine
1/3 cup venison stock (page 175) or beef broth
1/4 cup brandy
1/4 teaspoon dried thyme leaves

3 or 4 servings

Heat oven to 175°. On a sheet of waxed paper, mix flour, salt, and pepper. Dip liver slices in flour mixture, turning to coat. In large skillet, melt 1/4 cup butter over medium heat. Add liver slices; brown on both sides. With slotted spoon, transfer to heated serving platter. Keep warm in oven. Add onions to butter in skillet. Cook and stir over medium heat until tender. Set aside and keep warm.

While onions are cooking, place sugar on a sheet of waxed paper. Coat orange slices on both sides. In medium skillet, melt 1/4 cup butter over medium heat. Add orange slices. Fry until golden brown, turning once. Remove orange slices; set aside. Add stock, brandy, and thyme to butter in skillet. Cook over low heat for 5 minutes, stirring constantly. Remove from heat. To serve, arrange onions over liver slices. Pour broth mixture over onions and liver. Top with orange slices.

FRIED DEER HEART SLICES

1/4 cup all-purpose flour
1/4 teaspoon salt
1/8 teaspoon pepper

1 deer heart, sliced 1/4 inch thick
Vegetable oil or bacon
drippings

2 to 4 servings

On a sheet of waxed paper, mix flour, salt, and pepper. Dip heart slices in flour mixture, turning to coat. In medium skillet, heat 1/8 inch oil over medium heat until hot. Add heart slices. Fry until browned and cooked through, about 5 minutes, turning once.

VENISON HEART ROAST

1 deer or antelope heart,
    spiral sliced (see below)
1/2 cup all-purpose flour
1/2 teaspoon salt

1/8 teaspoon pepper
3 to 4 tablespoons bacon fat
4 or 5 slices bacon

3 or 4 servings

Heat oven to 325°. Mix flour, salt, and pepper on a sheet of waxed paper. Dip heart in flour mixture, turning to coat.

Heat bacon fat over medium-high heat in large skillet. Brown heart quickly on both sides. Remove from heat. Cool slightly. Lay 2 or 3 slices bacon on heart. Roll heart jelly-roll style, starting with the short end. Tie securely in two places with kitchen string. Place heart on rack in roasting pan. Cover with 2 slices bacon. Roast until heart is cooked through and tender, about 50 minutes.

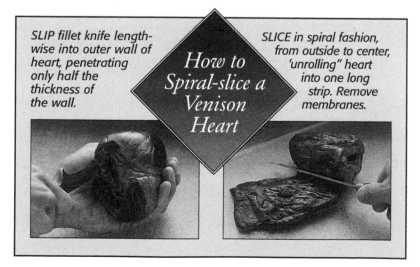

How to Spiral-slice a Venison Heart

SLIP fillet knife lengthwise into outer wall of heart, penetrating only half the thickness of the wall.

SLICE in spiral fashion, from outside to center, "unrolling" heart into one long strip. Remove membranes.

ITALIAN MEATBALLS AND SAUCE

SAUCE:
1 can (16 ounces) stewed
   tomatoes, undrained
1 can (6 ounces) tomato paste
1 cup burgundy
1 medium onion, chopped
2 cloves garlic, minced
3 tablespoons olive oil
1 can (15 ounces) tomato
   sauce
1 tablespoon Italian seasoning
1 tablespoon dried parsley
   flakes
1 teaspoon salt
1/2 teaspoon pepper

MEATBALLS:
6 slices dry French bread,
   crust removed
2 cups water
1 pound big-game burger
1 egg, slightly beaten
1 clove garlic, minced
1 teaspoon Italian seasoning
1/2 teaspoon dried basil leaves
2 tablespoons grated
   Parmesan cheese
1/2 teaspoon salt
1/8 teaspoon pepper
2 tablespoons bread crumbs,
   optional
3 tablespoons olive oil

Hot cooked spaghetti

4 to 6 servings

In food processor or blender, puree tomatoes. Blend in tomato paste and wine; set aside. In Dutch oven, cook and stir onion and 2 cloves minced garlic in oil over medium-high heat until tender. Add tomato mixture and remaining sauce ingredients. Heat to boiling. Reduce heat to low and cook until sauce thickens and flavors blend, about 2 hours, stirring occasionally.

To prepare meatballs: While sauce is cooking, in medium bowl, combine bread and water. Allow to stand 10 minutes. Drain bread; gently squeeze out excess water. Discard water. Crumble soaked bread into medium mixing bowl. Add meat, egg, 1 clove minced garlic, Italian seasoning, basil, cheese, salt and pepper. Mix well. If mixture is too soft to hold shape, add bread crumbs, 1 tablespoon at a time. Shape meat mixture into 16 meatballs, about 11/2 inches in diameter.

In medium skillet, heat 3 tablespoons oil over medium heat. Add meatballs; brown well on all sides, turning frequently. Remove meatballs with slotted spoon; drain on paper towels. Add meatballs to sauce during last hour of cooking. Serve meatballs and sauce over hot cooked spaghetti.

MEXICAN ENCHILADA CASSEROLE

2 pounds lean ground deer or other big game
1 medium onion, chopped
2 cloves garlic, minced
1 tablespoon vegetable oil, optional
1 can (8 ounces) tomato sauce
3 tablespoons chili powder
1/4 teaspoon salt
1 can (10 3/4 ounces) cream of chicken soup
3/4 cup milk
1 cup shredded Cheddar cheese
1 cup shredded Monterey Jack cheese
1 package (4.8 ounces) taco shells, coarsely crushed

8 to 10 servings

Heat oven to 350°. Grease 2-quart casserole; set aside. In large skillet, cook meat, onion, and garlic in oil over medium heat, stirring occasionally, until meat is no longer pink and onion is tender. Drain, if necessary. Stir in tomato sauce, chili powder, and salt. Heat over medium heat until bubbly. Reduce heat to very low; simmer for 10 minutes, stirring occasionally. Remove from heat; set aside.

In small mixing bowl, blend soup and milk; set aside. On a sheet of waxed paper, mix Cheddar and Monterey Jack cheeses; set aside.

In prepared casserole, layer one-third the crushed taco shells, half the meat mixture, half the soup mixture, and half the cheese mixture. Continue layering half the remaining taco shells, the remaining meat mixture, and the remaining soup mixture. Top with the remaining taco shells and the remaining cheese. Bake until hot in the center and cheese melts, about 45 minutes.

HUNTER'S FAVORITE CHILI

3 pounds big-game burger
3 medium onions, chopped
3 medium green peppers, chopped
1/2 cup chopped celery
2 tablespoons bacon fat or vegetable oil
1 can (28 ounces) whole tomatoes, undrained
2 tablespoons dried parsley flakes
2 tablespoons chili powder
1 teaspoon salt
1 teaspoon pepper
1/2 teaspoon garlic powder
2 cans (15 1/2 ounces) kidney beans, undrained
1 can (16 ounces) pinto beans, undrained

8 to 10 servings

In Dutch oven, brown meat over medium heat, stirring occasionally. Remove from heat and set aside. In large skillet cook and stir onions, green peppers, and celery in bacon fat over medium heat until tender. Add vegetable mixture and all remaining ingredients except beans to meat in Dutch oven. Heat to boiling. Reduce heat; cover. Simmer 1 hour to blend flavors. Stir in beans. Cook, uncovered, 30 minutes longer.

VENISON AND BEANS

6 slices bacon, chopped
1½ pounds deer, antelope, elk, or moose burger
1 medium onion, chopped
1 can (16 ounces) pork and beans
1 can (16 ounces) kidney beans, drained
1 can (16 ounces) butter beans or Great Northern beans, drained
⅓ cup packed brown sugar
1 cup catsup
2 tablespoons vinegar
1 tablespoon Worcestershire sauce
½ teaspoon salt
¼ teaspoon prepared mustard

8 to 10 servings

Heat oven to 350°. In Dutch oven, cook bacon over medium-low heat, stirring occasionally, until crisp. Remove with slotted spoon; set aside. Drain all but 1 tablespoon bacon fat from Dutch oven. Add meat and onion. Cook over medium heat, stirring occasionally, until meat is no longer pink and onion is tender. Add reserved bacon and remaining ingredients to Dutch oven; mix well. Cover and bake until bubbly around edges, about 45 minutes.

TEXAS-STYLE VENISON CHILI

1 to 1½ pounds boneless deer, moose, or elk
¼ cup all-purpose flour
3 tablespoons bacon fat or vegetable oil
2 medium onions, chopped
3 to 5 cloves garlic, minced
2 or 3 fresh green chilies, minced, or ½ to 1 teaspoon dried red pepper flakes
3 cans (16 ounces) whole tomatoes, undrained
1 teaspoon dried oregano leaves
1 teaspoon dried basil leaves
½ teaspoon ground cumin
1 medium green pepper, cut into ¾-inch chunks
Hot cooked rice

6 to 8 servings

Trim meat if necessary; cut into ½-inch cubes. Place meat cubes and flour in large plastic food-storage bag; shake to coat. In Dutch oven, lightly brown meat in bacon fat over medium-high heat, stirring frequently. Add remaining ingredients except green pepper and rice. Heat to boiling over medium heat. Boil gently for 15 minutes. Reduce heat. Simmer for 1 to 1½ hours, stirring occasionally. Add green pepper. Simmer for 30 minutes longer. Serve over hot cooked rice.

VENISON MEATBALL POT PIE

1 recipe single pie crust pastry
(page 154), or one pre-rolled,
refrigerated pie crust
1 package (5.5 ounces) au gratin
potatoes
1 package (10 ounces) frozen peas
and carrots, thawed and drained
1 pound lean ground deer,
antelope, elk, or moose
1 cup soft bread crumbs
1/4 cup milk
1 egg
2 tablespoons chopped onion
2 tablespoons snipped fresh
parsley
3/4 teaspoon salt
1/8 teaspoon pepper

4 to 6 servings

Heat oven to 375°. Prepare pie
crust dough as directed. Shape
into a ball. Wrap with plastic
wrap and refrigerate.

Prepare potatoes in 2-quart casserole according to package directions, omitting butter. Add peas
and carrots to cooked potatoes;
stir to combine. Set aside.

In large mixing bowl, combine
remaining ingredients. Mix well.
Shape into 16 meatballs, about 1 1/2
inches in diameter. Place meatballs
on top of potato mixture.

On lightly floured surface, roll out
crust slightly larger than top of
casserole, or smooth pre-made pie
crust as needed. Place crust on top
of casserole. Turn edge of crust
under; flute edge if desired. Cut a
small hole in the center of the crust
to allow steam to escape. Bake until
golden brown, 45 to 55 minutes.

SKILLET GAME HASH LOW-FAT

1 quart water
1/2 teaspoon salt
1 1/2 pounds potatoes
1 tablespoon butter
2 tablespoons vegetable oil
1/2 cup chopped onion
2 cups minced or ground
cooked big game
1 cup leftover thin game
gravy
1/2 teaspoon salt
1/4 teaspoon dried basil
leaves
1/4 teaspoon pepper
1/8 teaspoon dried thyme
leaves
Dash nutmeg
Dash garlic powder

4 to 6 servings

In medium saucepan, heat
water and 1/2 teaspoon salt
to boiling. Add potatoes.
Return to boiling. Reduce
heat; cover. Simmer until
tender, 20 to 25 minutes.
Cool. Peel and cut into
1/2-inch cubes.

In large skillet, melt butter
in oil over medium-high
heat. Add potatoes and
onion. Cook, stirring frequently, until potatoes are
lightly browned and onion
is tender. Remove from
heat. Add remaining ingredients. Mix well. Cover and
cook over low heat for 5
minutes to heat through
and blend flavors.

VENISON MEATLOAF SUPREME

2 pounds deer, antelope, elk, or moose burger
2 cups soft bread crumbs
1/2 cup venison stock (page 175) or beef broth
1/2 cup chopped onion
2 eggs, slightly beaten
1 teaspoon salt
1/2 teaspoon Worcestershire sauce
1/4 teaspoon sugar
1/4 teaspoon celery salt
1/4 teaspoon dried crushed sage leaves
1/4 teaspoon dried oregano leaves
1/4 teaspoon pepper
2 small tomatoes, peeled, halved, and seeded

6 to 8 servings

Heat oven to 325°. Grease 9 × 5-inch loaf pan; set aside. In large mixing bowl, combine all ingredients except tomatoes; mix well. Pat half of meat mixture into prepared pan. Arrange tomatoes on meat mixture, leaving 1/2 inch around edges of pan. Spread remaining meat mixture over tomatoes, pressing well around edges to seal. Bake until well browned, about 1 1/2 hours. Let stand 10 minutes. Remove to serving platter.

BIG-GAME PIE

DOUBLE PIE CRUST PASTRY:
- 2 cups all-purpose flour
- 1 teaspoon salt
- 2/3 cup shortening
- 3 tablespoons butter or margarine, room temperature
- 5 to 7 tablespoons cold water

FILLING:
- 2 cups cut-up cooked big game
- 1 1/2 cups thinly sliced potato
- 1/2 cup thinly sliced carrot
- 1/2 cup cubed rutabaga, 1/2-inch cubes
- 1 small onion, thinly sliced and separated into rings
- 1 package (.75 ounce) herb-flavored brown gravy mix, or 1 cup leftover game gravy
- 1/4 teaspoon salt
- 1/8 teaspoon pepper
- 1 tablespoon butter or margarine, cut up

GLAZE (OPTIONAL):
- 1 egg
- 1 tablespoon water

4 to 6 servings

Heat oven to 375°. Combine flour and salt in medium mixing bowl. Cut shortening and 3 tablespoons butter into flour until particles resemble coarse crumbs. Sprinkle flour mixture with cold water while tossing with fork, until particles just cling together. Divide into two balls. Roll one ball on lightly floured board into thin circle at least 2 inches larger than inverted 9-inch pie plate. Fit pastry into pie plate. Trim overhang. Set other ball aside.

Layer meat, potato, carrot, rutabaga, and onion in pastry

shell. Prepare gravy mix according to package directions, adding 1/4 teaspoon salt and the pepper. Pour into pie. Dot pie filling with butter.

Roll out remaining pastry. Place on filling. Seal and flute edges. If desired, roll out pastry scraps; cut into decorations and place on pastry top. Cut several slits in pastry top. In small bowl, blend glaze ingredients. Brush over pastry top. Bake until crust is golden brown, about 1 hour. Let stand 10 minutes before serving.

Big-Game Sausage

Fresh big-game sausage is surprisingly easy to make at home. All recipes in this section are for uncased sausages and require no special equipment other than a food processor or meat grinder.

You can use any big-game cut to make sausage. The best choices are cuts that might be tough if cooked whole. Scraps left after cutting up a big-game animal work well.

Fatty pork is usually added to the trimmed game meat to make sausage. If you prefer sausage with game meat only, you still need to add fat. Ask your butcher for hard pork or beef fat from the outside of the loin. A ratio of one part fat to three or four parts game meat produces a juicy, flavorful sausage. To produce the best texture, keep the fat and meat very cold during chopping or grinding.

Experiment with small batches to find a sausage recipe you like. Then double or triple the recipe to make a big batch. It's best to underseason sausage somewhat, then fry up a small patty and taste it. Add additional seasonings or salt if necessary.

Any of the sausage recipes in this book can also be used to make cased sausages. You'll need casings, available from some butcher shops, and a sausage stuffer. Follow the instructions that come with the stuffer.

Summer sausage and other cured or dried sausages are more difficult to make than the fresh sausages in this book. If you know how to make cured sausages, you can substitute game meat for beef.

Big-Game Sausage Recipes

SWEET ITALIAN SAUSAGE

This sausage can be used for pizza topping, meatballs, or break-fast patties. It also freezes well.

1 pound trimmed deer or other big-game meat
1 pound boneless fatty pork shoulder or
    pork butt
1 teaspoon salt
1 teaspoon sugar
1/2 teaspoon garlic powder
1/2 teaspoon fennel seed

1/2 teaspoon lemon pepper seasoning
1/2 teaspoon paprika
1/4 teaspoon celery salt
1/4 teaspoon dried crushed sage leaves
1/8 teaspoon cayenne
1 tablespoon soy sauce
1/2 teaspoon Worcestershire sauce

2 pounds

Cut the deer and pork into 3/4-inch cubes. Place in medium mixing bowl; set aside.

Mix remaining ingredients except soy sauce and Worcestershire sauce; sprinkle over meat. Toss to coat. Sprinkle soy and Worcestershire sauces over meat; mix. Cover. Refrigerate 8 hours or overnight.

Chop meat mixture to medium consistency in food processor, or grind with medium plate of meat grinder. Fry one small patty over medium heat to check seasoning. Adjust salt and other seasonings if necessary before cooking or freezing remaining sausage.

MEXICAN CHORIZO SAUSAGE

2 pounds trimmed deer or other big-game meat
2 pounds boneless fatty pork shoulder or pork butt
2 tablespoons paprika
1 tablespoon salt
1 tablespoon black pepper
2 teaspoons crushed red pepper flakes
1 teaspoon sugar
1 teaspoon garlic powder
1/2 teaspoon dried oregano leaves
1/4 teaspoon cumin seed
1/4 cup white vinegar

About 4 pounds

Cut deer and pork into 3/4-inch cubes. Place in large mixing bowl. In small bowl, mix remaining ingredients except vinegar. Sprinkle over meat; mix well. Chop or grind to medium consistency. Return meat mixture to large mixing bowl. Add vinegar; mix well. Cover bowl tightly with plastic wrap. Refrigerate for at least one hour to blend flavors. Cook over medium heat, stirring occasionally, until brown. Or, shape into tiny meatballs or patties, and fry over medium heat until browned and cooked through, turning to brown all sides. Sausage can also be frozen uncooked.

111

GARLIC SAUSAGE

  1 pound trimmed deer or other big-game meat
1½ pounds boneless fatty pork shoulder or pork butt
  3 to 4 teaspoons fresh minced garlic
  1 tablespoon salt
  1 teaspoon pepper
 ½ cup water

About 3 pounds

Cut deer and pork into ¾-inch cubes. Place in large mixing bowl. Sprinkle garlic, salt, and pepper over meat; mix well. Chop or grind to medium consistency. Return meat mixture to large mixing bowl. Add water; mix well. Cover bowl tightly with plastic wrap. Refrigerate for two days to blend flavors and allow garlic to mellow. Shape into thin patties and fry over medium heat until browned and cooked through, turning once. Sausage can also be frozen uncooked after two-day blending period.

POTATO SAUSAGE LOW-FAT

1 quart water
2 pounds peeled red potatoes
1 pound trimmed deer,
   antelope, elk, or moose
1 pound boneless fatty pork
   shoulder or pork butt
1 medium onion, coarsely
   chopped

1 egg, beaten
1 tablespoon salt
½ teaspoon ground allspice
¼ teaspoon dried ground sage
   leaves
¼ teaspoon dried basil leaves
¼ teaspoon sugar

4 pounds

In 2-quart saucepan, heat water to boiling. Add potatoes. Return to boiling. Reduce heat; cover. Simmer until potatoes are fork-tender, 25 to 35 minutes. Drain. Cool potatoes; cut into ¾-inch cubes.

Cut deer and pork into ¾-inch cubes. In large mixing bowl, combine deer, pork, potato cubes, onion, and egg. In small bowl, mix remaining ingredients. Sprinkle over meat and potato mixture; mix well. Cover bowl tightly with plastic wrap. Refrigerate at least 1 hour to blend flavors. Chop or grind meat and potato mixture to medium consistency. Shape into thin patties. Fry in nonstick skillet over medium-low heat in a small amount of vegetable oil until browned and cooked through, turning once. Leftover cooked sausage patties can be frozen.

VENISON BREAKFAST SAUSAGE

1 pound trimmed deer or other big-game meat
6 ounces lean bacon ends or slab bacon
3/4 teaspoon salt
1 teaspoon dried crushed sage leaves
1/2 teaspoon ground ginger
1/4 teaspoon pepper

1 1/2 pounds

Cut the deer and bacon into 3/4-inch cubes. Place in medium mixing bowl. In small bowl, mix salt, sage, ginger, and pepper. Sprinkle over meat; mix well. Chop or grind to desired consistency. Shape into thin patties and fry over medium heat until browned and cooked through, turning once. Sausage can also be frozen uncooked.

113

3

·················

SMALL GAME:

RECIPES

Cooking
Small Game

The species and age of a small-game animal determine the taste and texture of the meat. The taste and texture, in turn, determine the best cooking method. Squirrel meat is mild with a velvety texture. Young squirrels are delicious when fried; old ones would be tough if fried and are better stewed or simmered. Rabbits, because of their short life span, are usually tender and mild. Hares, whether young or old, are tougher and gamier.

To ensure tenderness, most of the recipes in this section rely on braising or other moist, slow-cooking methods. Pressure-cooking (page 119) also tenderizes quickly and easily, and is usually the best way to cook mature small-game animals.

To prepare a small-game dinner, you need about 3/4 pound of dressed game per person. Gray squirrels dress out at about 3/4 pound, fox squirrels 1 pound, cottontail rabbits 1 1/2 to 2 pounds and snowshoe hares 2 1/2 to 3 pounds.

SMALL GAME SUBSTITUTION

Because small game flavors vary, substituting one species for another may result in a dish that tastes quite different than the original. Also, hare is tougher than rabbit or squirrel, and requires longer cooking. Domestic rabbit will probably need less cooking time than wild rabbit.

If your recipe calls for a particular leftover or cooked small game, you can substitute any type of cooked small game, or even cooked pheasant, chicken, or turkey. Cuts of fresh upland game birds can be easily substituted for small game cuts of similar size, as well.

SMALL GAME SUBSTITUTION CHART

SPECIES	APPROXIMATE DRESSED WEIGHT	NUMBER OF SERVINGS	SUBSTITUTE	COOKING METHOD
Squirrel	¾ to 1 lb. (gray)	1	Cottontail rabbit (1 rabbit to 2 squirrels); Half of young snow- shoe hare; Portion of domestic rabbit; Pheasant or substi- tute (1 pheasant to 2 squirrels)	Panfry, braise, bake, stew, pressure- cook
	1 to 1½ lb. (fox)	1 to 1½		
Cottontail rabbit	1½ to 2 lbs.	2	2 squirrels; Young snowshoe hare; Portion of domestic rabbit; 1 pheasant or substitute	Panfry, bake, braise, stew, pressure- cook
Snowshoe hare	2½ to 3 lbs.	2 to 3	2 small cottontail rabbits; 2 to 3 squirrels; Domestic rabbit	Braise, stew, pressure- cook

PRESSURE COOKING TIMES FOR SMALL GAME

TYPE OF GAME	COOKING TIME (at 15 pounds pressure)
Squirrel, young	15 minutes
Squirrel, old	20 minutes
Cottontail rabbit	20 minutes
Snowshoe hare	25 minutes

Always follow the manufacturer's directions when using your pressure cooker. Consult the manual for specific recommendations. You may heat oil in your pressure cooker and brown the game before pressure-cooking, if desired. Add water carefully to the browned game, and seal the cooker immediately to prevent water loss.

HOW TO COOK SMALL GAME IN A PRESSURE COOKER

PLACE cut-up game in the pressure cooker, on a trivet if desired. Do not exceed two-thirds of the cooker's capacity. Add 1 to 1½ inches of water, or the amount specified in the cooker manual. Seal the cooker, then set the control for 15 pounds of pressure. Heat to full pressure as directed by the manual. Normally, the control starts to jiggle when full pressure is reached. Begin timing, then lower the heat so the control jiggles only one to four times per minute.

COOK as long as recommended by the chart (opposite page), then remove the cooker from the heat. Do not remove the control or open the cooker until it cools completely; escaping steam could cause serious burns. Cool according to the pressure-cooker manual. Generally, the cooker is allowed to cool naturally for about 5 minutes, then is placed under cold running water until it's cool enough to touch. Remove meat with tongs.

Small-Game Recipes

HOMESTEADERS' RABBIT OR SQUIRREL WITH CREAM GRAVY

3 tablespoons all-purpose flour
1/2 teaspoon salt
1/8 teaspoon pepper
1/8 teaspoon ground nutmeg
1 wild rabbit or 2 squirrels, cut up
2 tablespoons butter or margarine
2 tablespoons vegetable oil
3/4 cup rabbit stock (page 174) or chicken broth
1/2 cup chopped onion
1 small bay leaf
1/2 cup half-and-half

2 or 3 servings

In large plastic food-storage bag, combine flour, salt, pepper, and nutmeg; shake to mix. Add rabbit pieces; shake to coat. Reserve excess flour mixture. In large skillet, melt butter in oil over medium-low heat. Add coated rabbit pieces and excess flour mixture. Brown rabbit pieces on all sides over medium-high heat. Add stock, onion, and bay leaf. Heat to boiling. Reduce heat; cover. Simmer until meat is tender, 45 minutes to 1 hour for rabbit, about 1 1/2 hours for squirrel. Stir in cream. Cook over medium-low heat until cream is heated through; do not boil. Discard bay leaf before serving.

Variation: Follow recipe above, substituting 1/2 cup white wine and 1/4 cup water for the rabbit stock. Substitute 1/3 cup dairy sour cream for the half-and-half. Proceed as directed above.

↓ BRUNSWICK STEW

1/4 cup all-purpose flour
1 teaspoon salt
1/4 to 1/2 teaspoon pepper
3 squirrels, cut up
2 slices bacon, cut up
2 tablespoons butter or
  margarine
5 cups water
1 can (28 ounces) whole
  tomatoes, drained
1 medium onion, chopped

1 tablespoon packed brown
  sugar
2 medium potatoes
1 package (10 ounces) frozen
  lima beans
1 cup fresh or frozen
  whole-kernel corn
3 tablespoons all-purpose
  flour, optional
3 tablespoons cold water,
  optional

6 to 8 servings

In large plastic food-storage bag, combine 1/4 cup flour, the salt, and pepper; shake to mix. Add squirrel pieces; shake to coat. Set aside. In Dutch oven, combine bacon and butter. Heat over medium heat until butter melts. Add squirrel pieces; brown on all sides. Fry in two batches if necessary. Add 5 cups water, the tomatoes, onion, and brown sugar. Heat to boiling. Reduce heat; cover. Simmer until squirrel pieces are tender, 1 1/2 to 2 hours, stirring occasionally.

Remove squirrel pieces; set aside to cool slightly. Cut potatoes into 1/2-inch cubes. Remove squirrel meat from bones; discard bones. Add squirrel meat, potatoes, beans, and

corn to Dutch oven. Heat to boiling. Reduce heat; cover. Simmer until potatoes are tender, 25 to 35 minutes. If stew is thinner than desired, blend 3 tablespoons flour and 3 tablespoons cold water in small bowl. Add to stew, stirring constantly. Heat to boiling. Cook over medium heat, stirring constantly, until thickened and bubbly.

SHERRIED → SQUIRREL OR RABBIT

4 squirrels or 2 wild rabbits, cut up
2 quarts water
1 tablespoon salt
2 teaspoons vinegar
1/3 cup all-purpose flour
1 teaspoon salt
1/8 teaspoon pepper
2 tablespoons butter or margarine
2 tablespoons vegetable oil
8 ounces fresh whole mushrooms

SHERRY SAUCE:
1 cup rabbit stock (page 174) or chicken broth
1/4 cup sherry
1 tablespoon Worcestershire sauce
1/4 teaspoon seasoned salt
2 or 3 drops hot red pepper sauce

4 to 6 servings

In large glass or ceramic bowl, combine squirrel pieces, water, 1 tablespoon salt, and the vinegar. Cover bowl with plastic wrap. Let stand at room temperature 1 hour. Drain, discarding liquid. Pat squirrel pieces dry; set aside.

Heat oven to 350°. In large plastic food-storage bag, combine flour, 1 teaspoon salt, and the pepper; shake to mix. Add squirrel pieces; shake to coat. In large skillet, melt butter in oil over medium-low heat. Add squirrel pieces; brown on all sides over medium-high heat. Transfer squirrel pieces and drippings to 3-quart casserole. Add mushrooms. In 2-cup measure, combine all sherry sauce ingredients. Pour over squirrel pieces and mushrooms. Cover casserole. Bake until tender, about 1 1/2 hours.

SOUTHERN FRIED SQUIRREL OR RABBIT WITH GRAVY

1/3 cup all-purpose flour
1/2 teaspoon salt
1/8 teaspoon black pepper
1/8 teaspoon cayenne pepper, optional
2 squirrels or 1 wild rabbit, cut up
Vegetable oil

3 tablespoons all-purpose flour
1 1/2 cups milk or chicken broth
Salt and pepper
Brown bouquet sauce, optional

2 or 3 servings

In large plastic food-storage bag, combine 1/3 cup flour, the salt, black pepper, and cayenne pepper; shake to mix. Add squirrel pieces; shake to coat. In large skillet, heat 1/8 inch oil for squirrel, or 1/4 inch oil for rabbit, over medium-high heat until hot. Add coated meat; brown on all sides. Reduce heat; cover tightly. Cook over very low heat until tender, 35 to 45 minutes for squirrel, 20 to 25 minutes for rabbit, turning pieces once. Remove cover; cook 5 minutes longer to crisp. Transfer meat to plate lined with paper towels. Set aside and keep warm.

Discard all but 3 tablespoons oil. Over medium heat, stir 3 tablespoons flour into reserved oil. Blend in milk. Cook over medium heat, stirring constantly, until thickened and bubbly. Add salt and pepper to taste. Add bouquet sauce if darker color is desired. Serve gravy with meat.

OVEN-BARBECUED RABBIT

BARBECUE SAUCE:
- 2 medium onions, finely chopped
- 2 green peppers, finely chopped
- 1 clove garlic, minced
- 1 cup water
- 1 cup cider vinegar
- 1/2 cup catsup
- 1/2 cup packed brown sugar
- 1/4 cup butter or margarine, cut up
- 2 tablespoons Worcestershire sauce
- 1 teaspoon salt
- 1/2 teaspoon cayenne pepper

2 wild rabbits, cut up

4 to 6 servings

Heat oven to 300°. In medium saucepan, combine all barbecue sauce ingredients. Cook over medium-high heat until bubbly, stirring occasionally. Reduce heat. Simmer 10 minutes. Arrange rabbit pieces in single layer in 13 × 9-inch baking pan. Pour sauce evenly over rabbit pieces. Bake until tender, 2 1/2 to 3 hours, turning rabbit pieces occasionally.

RABBIT IN APPLE CIDER

1 tablespoon butter or margarine
1 tablespoon vegetable oil
1 wild rabbit, cut up
1 medium onion, cut into eighths
2 medium carrots, diced
1 1/2 cups apple cider
1/2 teaspoon salt
1/4 teaspoon dried thyme leaves
1 bay leaf
4 whole black peppercorns
2 medium cooking apples

2 or 3 servings

In Dutch oven, melt butter in oil over medium-low heat. Add rabbit pieces; brown well on all sides over medium-high heat. Remove rabbit pieces with slotted spoon; set aside. Add onion and carrots to oil. Cook and stir over medium heat until tender. Stir in cider, salt, thyme, bay leaf, and peppercorns. Heat to boiling. Add browned rabbit pieces. Reduce heat; cover. Simmer until rabbit pieces are tender, 50 minutes to 1 hour. Core and quarter apples. Add to rabbit pieces. Re-cover. Simmer until apples are just tender, 10 to 15 minutes. Discard bay leaf before serving. If desired, transfer rabbit pieces, vegetables, and apples to serving platter with slotted spoon.

RABBIT STEW

This recipe is pictured on the back cover.

1/4 cup olive oil
1 wild rabbit, cut up
1 medium onion, chopped
2 shallots, finely chopped
1 can (16 ounces) stewed tomatoes, undrained
1/2 cup red wine
1 1/2 cups sliced fresh mushrooms
2 medium carrots, sliced
2 tablespoons brandy
2 tablespoons snipped fresh parsley
1 teaspoon dried oregano leaves
1 teaspoon dried rosemary leaves
1/2 teaspoon salt
1/4 teaspoon pepper
1 cup pitted black olives

2 or 3 servings

In Dutch oven, heat oil over medium-high heat. Add rabbit pieces; brown on all sides. Remove rabbit pieces with slotted spoon; set aside. Add onion and shallots to oil. Cook and stir over medium heat until tender. Add browned rabbit pieces and remaining ingredients except olives. Mix well; cover. Cook over medium heat until rabbit is tender, 50 minutes to 1 hour, turning rabbit pieces occasionally. Add olives; re-cover. Cook about 10 minutes longer.

RABBIT BRAISED WITH BACON AND MUSHROOMS

8 slices bacon, cut up
1/3 cup all-purpose flour
1/2 teaspoon salt
1/8 teaspoon pepper
1 wild rabbit, cut up
2 tablespoons butter or margarine
1 cup red wine
1 medium onion, chopped

1/4 cup brandy
1/4 cup applesauce
1 tablespoon red wine vinegar
1 tablespoon Dijon mustard
2 cloves garlic, minced
1 1/2 cups sliced fresh mushrooms
Salt and freshly ground black pepper

2 or 3 servings

In large skillet, cook bacon over medium heat until crisp, stirring occasionally. Remove skillet from heat. Remove bacon with slotted spoon; set aside. Reserve 2 tablespoons bacon fat in skillet.

In large plastic food-storage bag, combine flour, salt, and pepper; shake to mix. Add rabbit pieces; shake to coat. Melt butter in reserved bacon fat in skillet over medium-low heat. Add coated rabbit pieces; brown well on all sides over medium-high heat. Remove rabbit pieces with slotted spoon. Add wine, onion, brandy, applesauce, vinegar, mustard, and garlic. Mix well. Return rabbit pieces to skillet. Heat to boiling. Reduce heat; cover. Simmer 45 minutes, turning rabbit pieces occasionally. Add mushrooms and cooked bacon. Re-cover. Simmer until rabbit pieces are tender, 10 to 20 minutes longer. Add salt and pepper to taste. Serve with buttered noodles, if desired.

HASENPFEFFER

1 hare or 2 wild rabbits, cut up

MARINADE:
2 cups red wine
1 cup water
1/2 cup cider vinegar
2 cloves garlic, minced
1/2 teaspoon dried thyme leaves
1/2 teaspoon dried rosemary leaves
1/2 teaspoon dried marjoram leaves
10 whole black peppercorns

1/2 cup all-purpose flour
6 slices bacon, cut up
8 ounces fresh mushrooms, cut into quarters
1 cup chopped onion
1 to 3 tablespoons butter
1 teaspoon salt
1/2 cup dairy sour cream

4 to 6 servings

In large glass or ceramic mixing bowl, combine hare pieces and all marinade ingredients. Cover bowl with plastic wrap. Refrigerate for 2 or 3 days, turning hare pieces daily.

Lift hare pieces out of marinade. Pat dry with paper towels; set aside. Strain and reserve 1 1/2 cups marinade, discarding herbs and excess marinade. Place flour on a sheet of waxed paper. Add hare pieces, turning to coat. In Dutch oven, cook bacon over medium heat until almost crisp. Add mushrooms and onion. Cook until onion is tender, stirring occasionally. Remove vegetable mixture with slotted spoon; set aside. Add 1 tablespoon butter to pan. Add hare pieces. Brown on all sides, adding additional butter if necessary. Return vegetable mixture to Dutch oven. Add salt and reserved marinade. Heat to boiling. Reduce heat; cover. Simmer until hare pieces are tender, 1 to 1 1/4 hours. With slotted spoon, transfer hare pieces to heated serving platter. Set aside and keep warm. Blend sour cream into cooking liquid. Cook over medium heat until heated through, stirring occasionally; do not boil. Serve sauce and hare with buttered noodles, if desired.

TUSCAN HARE WITH PASTA

1 hare, cut up
3 stalks celery, cut into
   2-inch pieces
3 carrots, cut into 2-inch pieces
1/2 teaspoon dried rosemary
   leaves
1 bay leaf
10 whole black peppercorns
2 tablespoons red wine vinegar
3 cups dry red wine
2 cups water

1/3 cup olive oil
1 large onion, chopped
2 cloves garlic, minced
1 can (16 ounces) whole
   tomatoes, undrained
1/4 cup tomato paste
2 teaspoons salt
   Hot cooked linguini or
   wide egg noodles
   Grated Parmesan cheese

4 to 6 servings

In Dutch oven, combine hare pieces, celery, carrots, rosemary, bay leaf, peppercorns, vinegar, wine, and water. Heat to boiling. Reduce heat; cover. Simmer for 45 minutes. Remove cover. Cook over medium heat for 1 1/2 hours longer. Remove hare pieces; set aside to cool slightly. Strain cooking liquid into 2-cup measure; discard vegetables. If there is more than 1 cup cooking liquid, boil in medium saucepan until reduced to 1 cup. If there is less than 1 cup cooking liquid, add water to equal 1 cup. Set cooking liquid aside. Remove hare meat from bones; discard bones. Shred meat coarsely with fingers.

In Dutch oven, heat oil over medium heat. Add shredded meat. Cook, stirring frequently, until meat begins to brown, about 5 minutes. Scrape browned bits from bottom of pan. Add onion and garlic; cook 10 minutes longer. Add reserved cooking liquid, tomatoes and juice, tomato paste, and salt. Heat to boiling. Reduce heat to medium. Cook until moderately thick, 30 to 45 minutes, stirring occasionally. Serve sauce over hot linguini; sprinkle with grated Parmesan cheese.

RABBIT OR SQUIRREL POT PIE

Follow recipe on page 154 for Savory Pot Pie, substituting 2 1/2 to 3 cups cut-up or shredded cooked rabbit or squirrel meat for the cooked turkey meat. Continue as directed.

FLORENTINE RABBIT PASTA

2 tablespoons butter or margarine
1 tablespoon minced fresh garlic
2 cups shredded cooked wild rabbit
2 cups whipping cream
1/4 cup snipped fresh parsley
1 teaspoon snipped fresh basil leaves or 1/2 teaspoon dried
   basil leaves
1/4 teaspoon white pepper
1/8 teaspoon ground nutmeg
1 package (12 to 16 ounces) spinach linguini
1/3 cup grated Parmesan cheese

4 to 6 servings

In medium skillet, melt butter over medium heat. Add garlic. Cook and stir until tender but not brown. Add rabbit meat. Cook and stir until hot. Stir in cream, parsley, basil, pepper, and nutmeg. Cook over low heat until liquid is reduced by one-third, 10 to 15 minutes.

While rabbit mixture is cooking, cook linguini according to package directions. Drain. Set aside and keep warm. When rabbit mixture is reduced, remove from heat. Stir in Parmesan cheese. Serve over hot cooked noodles.

4

UPLAND GAME BIRDS:
RECIPES

Cooking Upland Game Birds

Wild upland birds differ somewhat from their domestic counterparts, so different cooking techniques are required. Wild birds, for one thing, have much less fat. You can roast a whole wild turkey much as you would a domestic one, but you must baste it more often to keep the meat moist. And wild birds have more flavor; the best recipes are those that do not cover up the natural taste.

Exactly how to cook an upland game bird depends on its size, its age, the color of its meat, and whether it was plucked or skinned.

Turkey, pheasant, grouse, and partridge can be roasted much like domestic birds of the same size. Medium-sized upland birds like pheasant, grouse, and partridge can also be split and grilled, or cut up and fried or braised. Small upland birds like quail, woodcock, and dove are often baked in a covered casserole with liquid to keep them moist.

When dressing birds for the freezer, try to determine their age (page 50), then mark the packages accordingly. If the age is in doubt, it's best to cook with moist heat. Age is less important with small birds than with large ones.

On most upland birds, the breast meat is lighter in color

than the leg or thigh meat. But on some, the breast is dark as well. Light meat dries out more quickly and usually requires less cooking time than dark meat. By cutting birds up, you can cook each kind of meat exactly the right time. When packaging several birds for freezing, you may want to wrap the breasts and the legs in separate packages.

Plucked birds can be roasted whole or cut up and fried. The skin helps keep the meat moist during roasting, and when fried, it becomes crisp and tasty. Skinned birds are usually cut up and cooked with moist heat.

A wild turkey serves four to eight people, depending on its size. A pheasant serves two, and a pair of grouse serves three. Allow one partridge, two quail, or three woodcock or doves per person.

UPLAND GAME BIRDS SUBSTITUTION GUIDE

As with small game, there are noticeable differences in meat color and flavor among upland game birds. The subtle berry flavor of a ruffed grouse, for example, may be overpowered in a recipe with strong flavors, just as strong-flavored sharptail may not work in a lightly seasoned dish.

Game-farm birds, such as pheasants, chukar partridge, quail and turkey, can be easily substituted for wild birds in recipes. A game-farm bird will probably have more fat than a wild one, so remove the excess before cooking. Consult the chart at right for information on substituting one species for another.

UPLAND GAME BIRDS SUBSTITUTION CHART

SPECIES	APPROX. DRESSED WEIGHT	NUMBER OF SERVINGS	SUBSTITUTE	COOKING METHOD
Wild turkey (whole)	8 to 16 lbs.	5 to 10	Domestic turkey of similar weight (not prebasted type)	Oven roast
Wild turkey (any pieces)	3 to 4½ lbs	6 to 8	2 pheasants, quartered; 3 ruffed or sharptail grouse, halved; 3 or 4 chukar or Hungarian partridge, halved; 3 lbs. domestic turkey pieces, excess fat removed	Panfry, braise, bake
Pheasant (whole)	1½ to. 2¼ lbs.	3 to 4	2 ruffed or sharptail grouse; 2 chukar or Hungarian partridge	Oven roast, pan-broil, panfry, braise, bake
2 pheasants (cut up)	3 to 4½ lbs.	6 to 8	Thighs and legs from wild turkey; 3 or 4 ruffed or sharp-tail grouse, quartered; 4 chukar or Hungarian partridge, quartered; 8 quail, halved	Panfry, braise, bake
Pheasant (2 whole breasts, boneless)	1 lb.	4	Boned breast portion or thighs from turkey; Boned breast and thighs from 2 ruffed or sharp-tail grouse, 2 chukar or Hungarian partridge; Boned breasts from 4 quail; Boned breasts from 6 or 7 doves	Panfry, deep-fry, grill, braise, bake
Ruffed or sharptail grouse (whole)	1 to 1¼ lbs.	2 to 3	½ pheasant; 1 chukar or Hungarian partridge	Oven roast, panfry, bake, braise, grill
Chukar or Hungarian partridge	¾ to 1 lb.	2	½ pheasant; 1 ruffed or sharptail grouse	Oven roast, panfry, bake, braise
Quail	4 quail (4 to 6 oz. each)	4	1 pheasant, cut up; 1½ ruffed or sharptail grouse, cut up; 2 chukar or Hungarian partridge, quartered	Oven roast, panfry, bake, braise, grill
Woodcock	5 to 6 wood-cock, (5 oz. each)	4	1 pheasant, cut up; 1½ ruffed grouse, cut up; 2 chukar or Hungarian par-tridge, cut up; 4 quail, halved	Panfry, bake, braise
Dove	6 or 7 doves (2 to 3 oz. each)	4	1 pheasant, cut up, breast section halved; 1½ ruffed or sharptail grouse, cut up, breast sections halved; 2 chukar or Hungarian partridge, cut up, breast sections halved; 4 quail, halved	Panfry, braise, bake

ROASTING UPLAND GAME BIRDS

Birds with the skin on can be roasted in an open pan in a slow (325°) oven. Frequent basting helps keep the meat moist and makes the skin crisp and brown. Some cooks prefer roasting in oven cooking bags; the birds baste themselves, the skin browns well, and cleanup is easy.

Skinned birds should be handled differently. Moist cooking methods such as braising or steaming work better than open-pan roasting. If you choose to roast a skinned bird, cover the meat with strips of bacon, or rub it with softened butter and baste it frequently. Small birds like doves, quail, and woodcock can be wrapped in cabbage or grape leaves to retain moisture. Only young birds should be roasted. Older, tougher ones should be cooked with moist heat.

Insert a standard meat thermometer into the thigh of a turkey or pheasant before roasting, or check near the end of the roasting time with an instant-reading meat thermometer. Birds are done when the thigh temperature reaches 185°. If roasting smaller birds, test for doneness by wiggling the leg. When it moves freely, the bird is done. You can also prick the thigh; the juices should run clear. Don't prick too often or it will lose too much juice.

ROASTING TIMETABLE FOR WILD TURKEY

TURKEY	WEIGHT BEFORE STUFFING	APPROXIMATE COOKING TIME*
STUFFED	4 to 8 pounds	2 to 2¾ hours
	8 to 12 pounds	2½ to 3 hours
	12 to 15 pounds	3 to 3½ hours
	15 to 20 pounds	3½ to 4 hours
	20 to 25 pounds	4½ to 5 hours
UNSTUFFED	4 to 8 pounds	1¾ to 2¼ hours
	8 to 12 pounds	2 to 2½ hours
	12 to 15 pounds	2½ to 3 hours
	15 to 20 pounds	3 to 3½ hours
	20 to 25 pounds	4 to 4½ hours
*Roast at 350° to an internal temperature of 185°		

Upland Game Bird Recipes

ROAST WILD TURKEY

1 tablespoon all-purpose flour
1 medium onion, sliced
3 stalks celery with leaves, chopped
1 wild turkey, skin on, thawed completely
  Salt and pepper
1 recipe Apricot Stuffing (page 173) or other dressing (optional)
  Melted butter or margarine
2 tablespoons all-purpose flour
3 tablespoons cold water

Heat oven to 350°. Add 1 tablespoon flour to turkey-size (19 × 23 1/2-inch) oven cooking bag; shake to distribute. Place cooking bag in 13 × 9-inch roasting pan; add onion and celery. Season cavity of bird with salt and pepper; stuff lightly with dressing. Place any extra dressing in buttered casserole; cover and refrigerate. You can also roast turkey unstuffed.

Truss the turkey by tying its legs together over the body cavity with kitchen string. To prevent the wings from drying out during roasting, tuck the tips under the turkey's back. Brush entire turkey with melted butter; season with salt and pepper. Place turkey in oven cooking  bag with onion and celery. Close bag with provided nylon tie and place in roasting pan. Insert meat thermometer into thigh through top of oven cooking bag. Make six 1/2-inch slits in top of bag. Roast according to chart on opposite page. Bake extra dressing during the last 30 minutes. Remove turkey from bag; let sit for 20 minutes before carving.

For gravy: Blend 2 tablespoons flour into water. In saucepan, blend into drippings; cook over medium heat until thickened.

SUNDAY ROAST PHEASANT WITH DRESSING →

1 whole pheasant, skin on*
1 recipe Onion-Bread Dressing
   (page 172) or other dressing
2 tablespoons butter or
   margarine, melted
1/2 cup pheasant stock
   (page 174) or chicken broth

3 tablespoons all-purpose flour
1/4 cup milk
1 cup pheasant stock or
   chicken broth
Salt and pepper

3 or 4 servings

Heat oven to 325°. Stuff pheasant lightly with prepared dressing. Place remaining dressing in greased 1-quart casserole; cover and refrigerate. Place pheasant, breast-side up, in small roaster; brush with melted butter. Add 1/2 cup pheasant stock to roaster. Cover; roast for 30 minutes, basting once. Place casserole with extra dressing in oven; cook pheasant and dressing 20 minutes longer. Uncover roaster; increase temperature to 350°. Continue roasting pheasant and dressing until pheasant is tender and juices run clear, and dressing is heated through, 20 to 30 minutes longer, basting pheasant once.

Transfer pheasant to heated platter; keep warm. In small bowl, blend flour and milk. Add 1 cup pheasant stock to juices in roaster; heat to simmering on stove top. Blend in flour mixture; cook over medium heat, stirring constantly, until thickened and bubbly. Add salt and pepper to taste. Serve gravy with pheasant and dressing.

Variation: If pheasant is skinned, do not brush with melted butter. Instead, dust stuffed pheasant lightly with 2 tablespoons flour; place 3 slices bacon over pheasant. Continue as directed.

SUNDAY ROAST GROUSE WITH DRESSING

Follow pheasant recipe above, substituting 2 sharptail or ruffed grouse for pheasant. Stuff grouse lightly; brush with melted butter. Place grouse, breast-side up, in small roaster; add 1/2 cup stock. Cover. Roast grouse and extra dressing for 30 minutes, basting grouse once. Uncover roaster; increase temperature to 350°. Continue roasting grouse and dressing until grouse are tender and juices run clear, and dressing is heated through, 20 to 30 minutes longer, basting grouse once. Continue as directed.

SUNDAY ROAST PARTRIDGE WITH DRESSING

Follow pheasant recipe on page 138, substituting 3 Hungarian or chukar partridge for pheasant. Stuff partridge lightly; brush with melted butter. Place partridge, breast-side up, in small roaster; add 1/2 cup stock. Cover; roast for 45 minutes, basting once. Place casserole with extra dressing in oven. Uncover roaster; increase temperature to 350°. Continue roasting partridge and dressing until partridge are tender and juices run clear, and dressing is heated through, 30 to 45 minutes longer, basting partridge once. Continue as directed.

GRILLED MARINATED GAME BIRDS

2 whole pheasants or 4 whole partridge, skin on
1 recipe Lemon-Garlic Marinade (page 179) or other marinade
  Salt and freshly ground black pepper

4 servings

Split birds into halves with game shears (page 60). Place pheasant halves in large plastic food-storage bag. Pour prepared marinade over birds; seal bag. Refrigerate for at least 3 hours, or overnight, turning bag over occasionally.

Start charcoal briquets in grill. When briquets are covered with ash, spread them evenly in grill. Place grate above hot coals. Remove birds from marinade; reserve marinade. Arrange birds on grate, skin-side down. Grill until breasts are browned, 10 to 15 minutes, basting after every 5 minutes with reserved marinade. Turn birds over; continue grilling and basting until juices run clear when thigh is pricked. Remove from grill; season with salt and pepper.

BROILED MARINATED GAME BIRDS

Follow recipe above, cooking in preheated broiler instead of over charcoal. Arrange birds on broiler rack, skin-side down. Place rack 4 to 6 inches from heat. Broil until done, 20 to 35 minutes, turning once and basting several times.

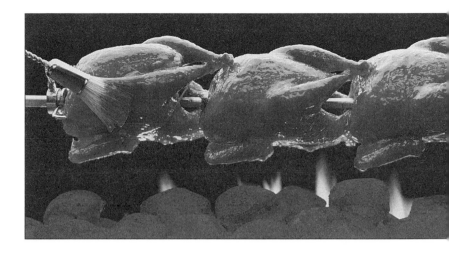

BARBECUED PARTRIDGE ON ROTISSERIE

1/2 cup hot pepper jelly
  1 cup prepared barbecue sauce
  2 to 4 whole partridge, skin on

2 to 4 servings

In small saucepan, cook hot pepper jelly and barbecue sauce over medium-low heat until sauce is hot and jelly melts, stirring constantly. Remove from heat; set aside and keep warm. Start charcoal briquets in rotisserie grill.

Tuck wing tips behind each bird's back. Tie drumsticks with wet kitchen string. Bring string along thigh, then between wing and body. Tie string behind bird's back.

Skewer birds on center of spit; secure with meat holders. If skewering three or four birds, you may skewer through ribs, changing direction of every other bird. Cook skewered birds on rotisserie over prepared charcoal, brushing with sauce mixture after the first 20 minutes and then after every 10 minutes. Test for doneness by pricking thigh; juices will run clear when done. Reheat remaining sauce if necessary; serve with birds.

UPLAND BIRDS IN OVEN COOKING BAG

1 tablespoon all-purpose flour
1/2 cup apple cider or orange juice
1 whole pheasant, or 2 grouse or partridge, skin on*
Salt
3 tablespoons melted butter or margarine
1/4 to 1/2 teaspoon bouquet garni seasoning or other herb mixture
1/2 apple

2 or 3 servings

Heat oven to 350°. Add flour to regular (10 × 16-inch) oven cooking bag; shake to distribute. Place bag in 10 × 6-inch baking dish and add cider; stir with plastic or wooden spoon to blend into flour. Salt body cavity of pheasant. Brush outside of bird with melted butter; sprinkle with herbs. Put 1/2 apple inside body cavity of pheasant (if cooking grouse or partridge, cut apple half into two pieces; place one piece inside cavity of each bird). Place pheasant in cooking bag and close with provided nylon tie. Make six 1/2-inch slits in top of bag. Roast until juices run clear when thigh is pricked, 1 to 1 1/4 hours. Slit bag down center and fold back. Continue cooking until pheasant is brown, about 15 minutes. Remove and discard apple. Stir juices and spoon over pheasant, if desired.

Variation: If birds are skinned, cover with 2 or 3 bacon strips if desired; omit butter.

QUAIL GRILLED IN CABBAGE LEAVES

1/2 cup butter or margarine
2 tablespoons snipped fresh parsley
1/4 teaspoon dried thyme leaves
1/4 teaspoon dried marjoram leaves
6 whole quail, skin on
6 large cabbage leaves*
Salt

3 servings

Start charcoal briquets in grill. Melt butter in small saucepan. Stir in parsley, thyme, and marjoram. Brush herb-butter mixture over outside of birds. Soak six 24-inch-long pieces of kitchen string in water. Wrap each bird in one cabbage leaf, folding ends of leaf in if leaves are large. Tie with wet string. Grill cabbage-wrapped birds over prepared charcoal for 15 minutes, turning frequently. Remove birds from grill. Carefully remove cabbage leaves; discard. Brush quail with herb-butter mixture. Grill unwrapped birds until golden brown and cooked through, 3 to 5 minutes, turning once. Salt lightly before serving.

To loosen leaves from cabbage head, cut out core. Place cabbage in bowl; cover with cold water. Let stand about 10 minutes; remove leaves.

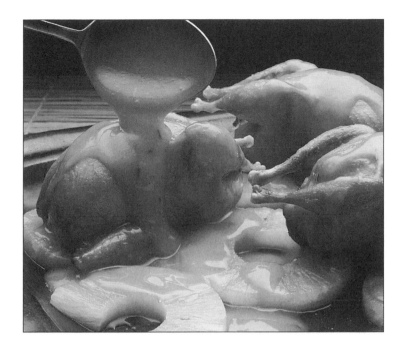

SAVORY PINEAPPLE-BAKED QUAIL

8 whole quail, skin on
1 can (20 ounces) sliced pineapple, drained, juice reserved
2 teaspoons Worcestershire sauce
2 teaspoons Dijon-style mustard
1 teaspoon dried rosemary leaves
1 tablespoon cornstarch
1 small lemon, thinly sliced
  Salt and pepper

4 servings

Heat oven to 400°. Arrange quail, breast-side down, in 10-inch-square baking dish or 3-quart casserole; set aside. In small mixing bowl, blend pineapple juice, Worcestershire sauce, mustard, rosemary, and cornstarch. Pour pineapple-juice mixture over quail. Bake, uncovered, for 20 minutes. Turn quail breast-side up; arrange pineapple and lemon slices over quail. Baste with sauce. Bake until quail are tender and juices run clear, 15 to 30 minutes longer. Arrange quail and pineapple slices on platter. Strain sauce if desired; salt and pepper to taste. Serve over quail.

DOVES IN CORN BREAD STUFFING

STUFFING:
1/2 cup chopped celery
1/4 cup sliced green onion
 2 tablespoons snipped fresh parsley
1/4 cup butter or margarine
 3 cups corn bread stuffing mix
 1 cup upland game bird stock (page 174) or chicken broth
1/2 teaspoon dried marjoram leaves
1/2 teaspoon salt
1/8 teaspoon pepper

 8 dove breasts

4 servings

Heat oven to 350°. Lightly grease 2-quart casserole; set aside. In medium skillet, cook and stir celery, onion, and parsley in butter over medium heat until tender. Add remaining stuffing ingredients. Mix until moistened. Place half of stuffing mixture in prepared casserole. Arrange dove breasts over stuffing. Cover completely with remaining stuffing mixture. Bake, uncovered, until dove is cooked through and tender, about 1 hour.

QUAIL IN CORN BREAD STUFFING

Follow recipe above, substituting 6 quail, split in half, for doves. Proceed as directed above.

HUNGARIAN HUNS

8 slices bacon, cut up
3/4 cup all-purpose flour
1 tablespoon paprika
3 or 4 Hungarian partridge
1/4 cup partridge stock (page 174) or chicken broth
3 tablespoons cider vinegar
1 small head green cabbage (about 1 1/2 pounds), very coarsely chopped
1 medium onion, coarsely chopped
1 apple, cored and cut into 1/2-inch cubes
1/2 teaspoon caraway seed
1/2 teaspoon salt
1/8 teaspoon pepper

4 to 6 servings

In Dutch oven, cook bacon over medium heat until crisp, stirring frequently. Remove from heat. Remove bacon with slotted spoon; set aside. Reserve 3 tablespoons bacon fat in Dutch oven.

In large plastic food-storage bag, combine flour and paprika; shake to mix. Add one partridge; shake to coat. Repeat with remaining partridge. Add partridge to bacon fat in Dutch oven; brown on all sides over medium-high heat. Add reserved bacon and remaining ingredients. Reduce heat; cover. Simmer until juices run clear when thigh is pricked, about 1 hour, rearranging birds and stirring vegetables once or twice.

WOODCOCK IN CHABLIS

 VERY FAST

6 to 8 woodcock breasts and legs, skinned
3 tablespoons butter or margarine
1 medium onion, thinly sliced
1 cup sliced fresh mushrooms
1 cup upland game bird stock (page 174) or chicken broth
1/2 cup chablis or dry white wine
3 tablespoons all-purpose flour
1/2 teaspoon salt
Dash pepper

2 to 4 servings

Bone woodcock breasts. Trim and discard any fat from breasts or legs. Discard fat and bones. In medium skillet, melt butter over medium heat. Add woodcock legs and boneless breast halves. Cook until woodcock has just lost its color. Remove woodcock from skillet with slotted spoon. Set aside.

Cook and stir onion in skillet over medium heat for 4 minutes. Add mushrooms. Cook and stir until vegetables are tender, 2 to 3 minutes. Return woodcock to skillet. In small bowl, blend remaining ingredients. Pour over woodcock and vegetables. Heat until bubbly, stirring constantly. Reduce heat; cover. Simmer until woodcock is tender, about 10 minutes, stirring once.

STEWED PARTRIDGE WITH SAGE DUMPLINGS

STEWED PARTRIDGE:
3 partridge, whole or cut up
1 1/2 quarts water
2 bay leaves
1 teaspoon dried thyme leaves
1 teaspoon dried rosemary leaves
1 teaspoon dried summer savory leaves, optional
2 teaspoons salt
1/8 teaspoon freshly ground black pepper
4 carrots, cut into 1-inch chunks
3 stalks celery, cut into 1-inch chunks
2 medium onions, cut into wedges

SAGE DUMPLINGS:
1 1/2 cups all-purpose flour
2 teaspoons baking powder
1/2 teaspoon salt
1/2 to 3/4 teaspoon crushed sage
2/3 cup milk
3 tablespoons butter or margarine, melted

4 to 6 servings

In Dutch oven, combine partridge, water, bay leaves, thyme, rosemary, and savory. Heat to boiling. Reduce heat; cover. Simmer for 1 1/2 hours. Add 2 teaspoons salt, the pepper, carrots, celery, and onions; cook until partridge and vegetables are tender, about 45 minutes. Remove from heat. Remove partridge and bay leaves from stock and vegetables; discard bay leaves. Cool partridge slightly.

Skim fat from broth. Remove partridge meat from bones and any skin. Tear meat into bite-size pieces and return to broth. Discard bones and skin.

To make dumplings, in medium mixing bowl, combine flour, baking powder, 1/2 teaspoon salt, and the sage; stir with fork to combine. Add milk and melted butter; stir until flour is moistened. Set aside.

Heat meat, vegetables, and broth until broth boils. Drop dumpling dough by heaping tablespoons onto broth mixture. Cook over medium-high heat for 5 minutes; cover and cook until dumplings are firm, about 10 minutes longer.

BAKED PHEASANT IN MADEIRA

1 pheasant, cut up
Salt
¼ pound fresh mushrooms
1 tablespoon chopped onion or 1 teaspoon minced dried onion
1 cup pheasant stock (page 174) or chicken broth
1 cup Madeira wine
1 teaspoon lemon juice
1 tablespoon cornstarch
2 tablespoons cold water

2 or 3 servings

Heat oven to 325°. Sprinkle pheasant pieces lightly with salt; place in Dutch oven. Add mushrooms, onion, stock, wine, and lemon juice. Cover; bake until pheasant is tender, 1½ to 2½ hours. Transfer pheasant and mushrooms to heated platter with slotted spoon. Set aside and keep warm.

In small bowl, blend cornstarch and water. Blend into cooking liquid in Dutch oven. Heat to boiling, stirring constantly. Cook, stirring constantly, until thickened and translucent. Serve over pheasant.

PHEASANT IN CREAMY MUSHROOM SAUCE

1 can (10¾ ounces) condensed cream of mushroom soup
½ cup dairy sour cream
¼ cup milk
2 tablespoons sherry, optional
½ cup all-purpose flour
1 teaspoon salt
¼ teaspoon pepper
2 pheasants, cut up
¼ cup vegetable oil
8 ounces fresh whole mushrooms
1 medium onion, cut into 8 chunks
¼ teaspoon dried thyme leaves, optional

4 to 6 servings

Heat oven to 300°. In small mixing bowl, blend soup, sour cream, milk, and sherry; set aside. In large plastic food-storage bag, combine flour, salt, and pepper; shake to mix. Add pheasant pieces; shake to coat. In Dutch oven, heat oil over medium-high heat. Add pheasant pieces; brown on all sides. Brown pieces in two batches if necessary. Return all pheasant to Dutch oven. Add mushrooms, onion, thyme, and reserved soup mixture. Cover. Bake until pheasant is tender, 1½ to 2 hours.

Variation: Follow recipe above, omitting the soup, sour cream, milk, and sherry. Reserve 3 tablespoons of seasoned flour after coating pheasant. After browning pheasant pieces, remove from Dutch oven. Remove Dutch oven from heat. Stir in reserved flour. Add 2 cups half-and-half. Cook over medium-low heat, stirring constantly, just until mixture bubbles. Return pheasant pieces to pan. Add mushrooms, onion, and thyme. Cover; bake as directed above.

PHEASANT PAPRIKA

8 slices bacon, cut up
1/4 cup chopped onion
1 1/2 cups instant mashed potato flakes
1 1/2 teaspoons paprika
1 1/2 teaspoons salt
2 to 3 pounds pheasant pieces
1/4 to 1/2 cup pheasant stock (page 174) or chicken broth
2 tablespoons butter or margarine
2 tablespoons all-purpose flour
1 cup pheasant stock or chicken broth
2/3 cup milk
1 tablespoon paprika
1 to 1 1/2 cups dairy sour cream
    Hot cooked egg noodles

4 to 6 servings

In medium skillet, cook bacon over medium heat until it just begins to brown. Add onion. Cook and stir until onion is tender. Remove from heat. With slotted spoon, remove bacon and onion from skillet. Set bacon and onion aside; reserve drippings.

In large plastic food-storage bag, combine potato flakes, 1 1/2 teaspoons paprika, and salt; shake to mix. Add pheasant, a few pieces at a time, to bag; shake to coat. In reserved drippings, brown pheasant pieces over medium-high heat. Add 1/4 cup stock to pan. Reduce heat; cover. Simmer until tender, 25 to 40 minutes, adding the additional 1/4 cup stock to pan during cooking if necessary.

To prepare sauce: In 1-quart saucepan, melt butter over medium heat. Stir in flour. Blend in 1 cup stock. Cook, stirring constantly, until thickened and bubbly. Stir in milk, 1 tablespoon paprika, and reserved bacon and onion. Cook and stir until hot. Pour sauce over cooked pheasant in skillet. Cover and simmer 10 to 15 minutes. Remove from heat; skim fat. With slotted spoon, transfer pheasant to serving platter; keep warm. Stir sour cream into mixture in skillet. Cook over low heat until just heated; do not boil. Pour sauce over pheasant. Serve with hot cooked egg noodles.

SHARPTAIL ON MUSHROOM TOAST FAST →

1/4 cup dry red wine
1/4 cup grouse stock (page 174) or chicken broth
1 1/2 teaspoons all-purpose flour
1/4 teaspoon dry mustard
1/4 teaspoon salt
4 tablespoons butter or margarine
4 slices French bread, 3/4 inch thick and 5 to 6 inches across
1 tablespoon chopped shallot
1 tablespoon butter or margarine
8 ounces fresh mushrooms, very finely chopped
  Salt and freshly ground black pepper
1 tablespoon butter or margarine
1 tablespoon vegetable oil
4 boneless breast halves from 2 sharptail grouse
2 teaspoons snipped fresh parsley, optional

4 servings

In small bowl, blend wine, stock, flour, dry mustard, and 1/4 teaspoon salt; set aside. In medium skillet, melt 2 tablespoons butter. Add 2 slices bread; turn quickly to coat both sides with melted butter. Cook over medium heat until golden brown on both sides. Repeat with remaining bread slices and 2 tablespoons butter; set aside and keep warm.

In medium skillet, cook and stir shallot in 1 tablespoon butter over medium heat until tender. Add chopped mushrooms. Cook over medium heat, stirring frequently, until the liquid has cooked off, about 10 minutes. Remove from heat. Salt and pepper to taste; set aside and keep warm.

In another medium skillet, melt remaining 1 tablespoon butter in oil over medium-low heat. Add breast halves. Cook over medium heat until well-browned on both sides but still moist in the center, about 10 minutes. Remove from skillet. Set aside and keep warm. Stir reserved wine mixture; blend into cooking juices in skillet. Cook and stir over medium heat until thickened and bubbly. Remove from heat; stir in parsley.

Spread each toast slice with one-fourth of the reserved mushroom mixture. Quickly slice each breast half into thin diagonal slices; arrange on mushroom toast. Drizzle about 2 tablespoons wine sauce over each portion.

STUFFED BREASTS OF GROUSE

8 boneless breast halves from 4 grouse
8 slices bacon
1 recipe Onion-Bread Dressing (page 172)
3 tablespoons grouse stock (page 174) or chicken broth
1 recipe Dried Mushroom Sauce (page 177), optional

4 servings

Heat oven to 350°. Prepare Onion-Bread Dressing as directed, adding additional 3 tablespoons stock. Place one-fourth of the dressing on each of four breast halves. Top with remaining four breast halves. Wrap 2 slices bacon around each breast-and-stuffing bundle. Secure bacon slices with toothpicks. Arrange bacon-wrapped bundles in 8-inch-square baking dish. Cover baking dish with aluminum foil. Bake for 45 minutes. Remove foil, and bake for 15 minutes longer. Transfer to serving platter or individual plates. Spoon sauce over each serving.

UPLAND STIR-FRY FAST

1 cup buttermilk baking mix
1/2 teaspoon pepper
3/4 to 1 pound diced uncooked pheasant or other upland bird
2 eggs, slightly beaten
1 tablespoon peanut oil
3 medium carrots, cut diagonally into 1/2-inch pieces
1 green pepper, cut into strips
1 small onion, thinly sliced and separated into rings
2 tablespoons water
3 tablespoons peanut oil
3/4 cup chicken broth
2 tablespoons teriyaki sauce
   Hot cooked rice

4 to 6 servings

In large plastic food-storage bag, combine baking mix and pepper; shake to mix. Set aside. In large mixing bowl, combine pheasant meat and eggs; stir to coat meat with egg. Remove pheasant from bowl with slotted spoon; transfer to plastic bag with baking mix. Shake to coat. Remove pheasant from bag; set aside. Discard excess baking mix and egg.

In wok or large skillet, heat 1 tablespoon oil over medium-high heat until hot. Add carrots; cook and stir for about 2 minutes. Add green pepper and onion. Cook and stir for 1 minute longer. Add water; cover. Steam for 3 to 4 minutes, until vegetables are tender-crisp. Remove vegetables from wok and keep warm.

Add 3 tablespoons oil to wok; heat over medium-high heat until hot. Add pheasant; cook and stir until golden brown and no longer pink in center. Combine chicken broth and teriyaki sauce; pour over meat. Return vegetables to wok. Cook and stir until heated through. Serve with rice.

WILD TURKEY PICATTA WITH MORELS

Half of wild turkey breast, skin and bones removed
2 cups milk
1 cup all-purpose flour
1/2 teaspoon salt
1/4 teaspoon paprika
   Dash pepper
4 to 6 tablespoons butter or margarine
3/4 cup coarsely chopped fresh morels*
3 tablespoons butter or margarine
2 tablespoons coarsely chopped fresh chives
   Salt and freshly ground black pepper

4 or 5 servings

Cut turkey breast into 1/2-inch-thick slices across the grain. Place a slice on a cutting board between two sheets of waxed paper. Pound gently to 1/4-inch thickness with saucer or flat side of meat mallet. Repeat with remaining slices. Place turkey slices in 12 × 8-inch baking dish. Add milk. Let stand at room temperature for 30 minutes. Remove turkey slices. Place milk in small bowl; set aside.

Heat oven to 175°. In large plastic food-storage bag, combine flour, salt, paprika, and pepper; shake to combine. Remove 3 tablespoons flour mixture; stir into reserved milk. Set aside. Add one turkey slice to remaining flour mixture in bag. Shake gently to coat. Remove and repeat with remaining slices. In medium skillet, melt 4 tablespoons butter over medium heat. Add half the turkey slices. Cook until golden brown and cooked through, turning once. Transfer turkey slices to heated platter; keep warm in oven. Add additional butter to skillet, if necessary. Repeat with remaining turkey slices.

In medium skillet, cook and stir mushrooms in 3 tablespoons butter over medium heat until tender. Stir in reserved milk mixture and chives. Cook over medium heat, stirring constantly, until thickened and bubbly. Salt and pepper to taste. If necessary, blend in additional milk to desired consistency. Serve sauce over turkey slices.

Variation: Substitute 1/2 ounce dried morels, available at specialty food stores, for fresh morels. Place dried morels in plastic bag. Add 1/4 cup hot water. Squeeze out excess air; seal bag with tie. Set aside to rehydrate for about 15 minutes.

SAVORY POT PIE

SINGLE PIE CRUST PASTRY:
 1 cup all-purpose flour
 1/4 teaspoon salt
 1/2 cup shortening
 2 to 4 tablespoons cold water

FILLING:
 2 tablespoons butter or margarine
 1/2 cup water
 1 cup thinly sliced carrot
 1 medium potato, cut into 1/4-inch cubes
 1/2 cup thinly sliced celery
 1/2 cup chopped onion
 1/2 cup frozen peas
 2 1/2 to 3 cups cut-up cooked turkey, pheasant or partridge
 1 recipe Dried Mushroom Sauce (page 177)
 1 egg yolk, slightly beaten

4 to 6 servings

Heat oven to 375°. To prepare pastry: In medium mixing bowl, combine flour and salt. Cut shortening into flour until particles resemble coarse crumbs or small peas. Sprinkle with cold water while tossing with fork, until particles are just moist enough to cling together. Shape into a ball. Wrap with plastic wrap and refrigerate.

In medium saucepan, combine butter and water. Heat until butter melts. Add carrot; cover and cook over medium heat for 3 minutes. Add potato; re-cover and cook for 5 minutes longer, stirring twice. Add celery, onion, and peas; re-cover and cook for 3 minutes, stirring once. Drain vegetable mixture. In medium mixing bowl, combine vegetable mixture, cooked meat, and prepared sauce. Stir well to mix. Transfer mixture to 1 1/2-quart casserole.

On lightly floured surface, roll out pastry slightly larger than top of casserole. Place pastry on top of casserole. Turn edge of pastry under; flute edge if desired. Brush pastry with beaten egg yolk. Cut a small hole in center of pastry to allow steam to escape. Bake until golden brown, 30 to 35 minutes.

TURKEY LENTIL SOUP LOW-FAT

1 turkey carcass, fairly meaty
8 cups water
1 medium onion, quartered
1/4 cup snipped fresh parsley
1 clove garlic, minced
2 teaspoons salt
1/4 teaspoon dried marjoram leaves
1/4 teaspoon pepper
1/8 teaspoon dried thyme leaves
1 cup thinly sliced carrot
3/4 cup dried lentils
1/2 cup thinly sliced celery
1/2 teaspoon salt
   Dash pepper

2 quarts

In Dutch oven, combine turkey carcass (cut up if desired), water, onion, parsley, garlic, 2 teaspoons salt, marjoram, 1/4 teaspoon pepper, and thyme. Heat to boiling. Reduce heat; cover. Simmer until meat on bones is very tender, 1 1/2 to 2 hours. Strain broth through several layers of cheesecloth; reserve broth. Remove meat from carcass; discard carcass and any skin. Return broth and meat to Dutch oven. Stir in remaining ingredients. Heat to boiling. Reduce heat; cover. Simmer until lentils are tender, about 30 minutes.

5

WATERFOWL:
RECIPES

Cooking Waterfowl

For many lucky families, roast wild goose is the traditional holiday fare. Dedicated waterfowlers think nothing of setting out hours before dawn, then waiting in the cold and damp for a chance at a magnificent Canada goose to grace the Thanksgiving or Christmas table.

Wild geese and ducks are more robustly flavored than domestic waterfowl. They're delicious if properly prepared, although the dark, rich meat is not to everyone's liking. Geese have a milder flavor than ducks, and may be a better choice for serving to those who have never tasted wild waterfowl.

The taste of ducks varies greatly, depending on the species and the individual duck. Canvasbacks, ringnecks, mallards, and teal are the favorites for eating. Redheads, black ducks, wood ducks, and pintails also are excellent. But a duck's diet affects the taste, so there's some variation within any species.

Smell the meat before cooking it. If it has a muddy or fishy odor, you may wish to marinate it or cook it with a flavorful sauce.

Next, consider the fat content of each duck you take. One that's just begun its winter migration will have more fat than one that's recently flown a long distance. As ducks recuperate from migration, they begin to build up fat again. One taken on its wintering area in the late season will be plumper than one taken earlier.

The breast is the best place to check for fat. If you can see a yellow layer through the skin, the duck is fat enough for roasting. Another option is smoking. Scaup, ringnecks, goldeneyes, and other diving ducks are especially good for this, since they usually have more fat than mallards, teal, wood ducks, and other puddle ducks. If the duck's breast skin appears dark, however, it may lack fat. Lean ducks require more basting, or moist cooking.

Also, consider the bird's age (page 50). Old, tough birds can be tenderized by long, moist cooking, by parboiling and then roasting, or by pressure-cooking. To pressure-cook, first remove the skin and excess fat. Cut a large bird into pieces to fit the cooker; smaller birds can be cooked whole. Follow the directions on page 119, cooking 20 to 25 minutes at 15 pounds pressure. The pressure-cooked meat is excellent in casseroles and salads.

Some people enjoy their duck cooked rare. The meat is juicy and flavorful, slightly reminiscent of rare beef. At the other extreme, some prefer it cooked at low heat until the meat literally falls off the bone.

To determine degree of doneness, prick the bird with a fork. If the juices are rosy, the bird is rare. The meat will be slightly springy to the touch; internal temperature will be 145° to 150°. Well-done birds read 180°; juices will run clear. The drumstick should wiggle freely in the joint.

Larger ducks, such as mallards, canvasbacks, black ducks, and redheads, will serve two people each. Gadwalls, widgeons, wood ducks, pintails, ringnecks, scaups, and goldeneyes are smaller; three ducks will serve four. Allow one teal per person. A Canada goose will serve from three to eight people, depending on its size. Blue geese, snow geese, and white-fronted geese are smaller than most Canadas, and usually serve two to six each.

WATERFOWL SUBSTITUTION GUIDE

With over 20 species of ducks and geese on this chart, we've taken a "mix-and-match" approach to substitutions. The chart is broken into four areas: Large Geese, Medium-size Geese, Small Geese/Large Ducks and Small Ducks. If the recipe calls for a mallard, locate it on the chart, then substitute any of the other ducks from that same area of the chart.

Breast meat from any of these birds can be substituted for mallard breast in recipes. Domestic ducks are generally too fatty to substitute for wild ducks. Upland game birds with dark meat also make good substitutes for duck if the cuts are the same size.

If a recipe calls for a whole Canada goose, you can substitute any wild goose of similar size. You can also substitute a domestic goose of the proper size, but the flavor is not as rich as that of wild goose. You will have to prick the skin of a domestic goose frequently during roasting to allow the excess fat to drain off; skim the fat from the pan juices prior to making gravy or sauce.

WATERFOWL SUBSTITUTION CHART

SPECIES		APPROX. DRESSED WEIGHT	NUMBER OF SERVINGS	COOKING METHOD
LARGE GEESE	Giant Canada (young)	4 to 6 lbs.	4 to 6	oven roast, grill, panfry
	Giant Canada (mature)	6½ to 10 lbs.	6 to 10	parboil/roast, braise, stew
	Interior Canada (mature)	4¾ to 6 lbs.	5 to 10	parboil/roast, braise, stew
MEDIUM-SIZE GEESE	Lesser Canada Goose	3 to 4½ lbs.	3 to 6	
	Snow or Blue Goose	3 to 4 lbs.	3 to 5	oven roast, grill, panfry
	White-fronted Goose	3½ to 3¾ lbs.	3 to 5	
	Interior Canada (young)	3½ to 4½ lbs.	4 to 5	
SMALL GEESE/ LARGE DUCKS	Cackling Canada	2 to 2½ lbs.	2 to 3	
	Brant	1¾ to 2½ lbs.	2 to 3	
	Canvasback	1¾ lbs.	2	
	Mallard	1¼ to 1½ lbs.	2	oven roast, grill, panfry
	Black Duck	1¼ to 1½ lbs.	2	
	Redhead	1¼ lbs.	2	
	Greater Scaup (Bluebill)	1¼ lbs.	2	
SMALL DUCKS	Goldeneye (Whistler)	1 to 1¼ lbs.	1 to 1½	
	Pintail	1 to 1¼ lbs.	1 to 1½	
	Gadwall	¾ to 1 lb.	1 to 1½	
	Lesser Scaup	¾ to 1 lb.	1 to 1½	
	Widgeon (Baldpate)	¾ to 1 lb.	1 to 1½	
	Ringneck (Ringbill)	¾ lb.	1 to 1½	oven roast, grill, panfry
	Wood Duck	½ to ¾ lb.	1	
	Bufflehead	5 oz. to ¾ lb.	1	
	Blue-winged Teal	½ lb.	1	
	Cinnamon Teal	5 oz. to ½ lb.	1	
	Green-winged Teal	5 to 6 oz.	1 or less	

Waterfowl Recipes

STUFFED ROAST GOOSE
Prepare a young goose with this traditional recipe.

1 whole wild Canada goose, 3 to 5 pounds, skin on
   Salt and pepper
1 recipe Apricot Stuffing (page 173) or other dressing

3 to 5 servings

Heat oven to 400°. Sprinkle cavity of goose lightly with salt and pepper. Stuff lightly with Apricot Stuffing. Tuck wing tips behind back. Tie drumsticks across cavity. Place goose, breast-side up, on rack in roasting pan. Sprinkle lightly with salt and pepper. Roast for 1 hour, basting with pan juices frequently. Drain and discard excess fat during roasting. Reduce oven temperature to 325°. Roast until goose is desired doneness, 1 to 1½ hours longer, basting frequently.

"POACHED" WILD GOOSE
Although this recipe may sound illegal, the title refers to the cooking technique, not the method of procurement. Use this recipe if you have a mature goose to cook.

1 whole wild goose, skin on
1 large onion, quartered
2 stalks celery, cut into 1-inch pieces
2 carrots, cut into 1-inch pieces
1 bay leaf
   Hot water
2 tablespoons butter or margarine, melted

4 to 8 servings

In large stockpot, combine goose, onion, celery, carrots, and bay leaf. Add water to cover. Heat to boiling. Reduce heat. Simmer until tender, 1½ to 2½ hours; if size of goose prohibits covering with water, turn goose over once or twice during cooking. Heat oven to 400°. Drain goose; strain broth and save for other recipes. Pat goose dry. Place in roasting pan. Brush with melted butter. Roast until skin is brown and crisp, 20 to 30 minutes.

ROAST GOOSE WITH BAKED APPLES

BAKED APPLES:
  6 to 8 firm medium
    apples, cored
  1 cup mashed
    cooked sweet
    potatoes
  1/4 cup packed brown
    sugar
  2 tablespoons butter
    or margarine,
    melted
  1/4 teaspoon salt
    Dash pepper

  1 whole wild goose, 6 to 8 pounds, skin on
    Seasoned salt
    Salt and pepper
  1 carrot, cut into 1-inch pieces
  1 stalk celery, cut into 1-inch pieces
  1 medium onion, cut into 8 pieces
    Apple brandy or Calvados, optional

6 to 8 servings

Remove a thin strip of peel from the top of each apple. In medium mixing bowl, combine remaining apple ingredients. Mix well. Stuff apples with sweet potato mixture, mounding on top. Place in shallow baking dish. Set apples aside.

Heat oven to 325°. Pat goose dry with paper towels. Sprinkle cavity lightly with seasoned salt, salt, and pepper. Place carrot, celery, and onion in cavity. Tie drumsticks across cavity. Tuck wing tips behind back. Place, breast-side up, on rack in roasting pan. Sprinkle outside of goose with seasoned salt, salt, and pepper. Roast, basting frequently with pan juices and sprinkling occasionally with brandy, until desired doneness, 20 to 25 minutes per pound. Drain and discard excess fat during roasting.

Place stuffed apples in oven during last 30 to 45 minutes of roasting. Baste apples frequently with goose drippings. Remove apples when fork-tender; serve with goose.

POLYNESIAN ROAST DUCK

4 mallards or other large wild
  ducks, or 6 to 8 smaller
  wild ducks, skin on or
  skinned
2 quarts water
3/4 pound mild pork sausage
1 cup chopped green pepper
3/4 cup chopped celery
1/3 cup chopped onion
4 cups cooked white, brown,
  or mixed rice
1 can (20 ounces) crushed
  pineapple, drained

1/2 teaspoon salt
1/4 teaspoon pepper
1/4 cup packed brown sugar
1/4 cup white wine

SAUCE:
  3 tablespoons cider vinegar
  2 tablespoons cornstarch
1 1/2 cups fresh orange juice
  1/4 cup granulated sugar
  1/2 teaspoon salt
  Dash pepper

8 servings

In Dutch oven, combine ducks and water. Heat to boiling.
Reduce heat. Simmer 45 minutes for large ducks, 30 minutes for smaller ducks. Drain, reserving broth. Set ducks
aside. Skim fat and strain broth. Reserve 1 cup broth for
sauce. Save remaining broth for use in other recipes.

Heat oven to 350°. Grease a 13 × 9-inch baking pan; set
aside. In large skillet, cook and stir sausage, green pepper,
celery, and onion over medium heat until sausage is
brown and vegetables are tender. Drain. In large mixing
bowl, combine sausage mixture, rice, pineapple, salt, and
pepper. Mix well. Stuff ducks lightly. Spoon remaining rice
mixture into baking pan. Arrange ducks on rice. In small
saucepan, combine brown sugar and wine. Heat to boiling,
stirring occasionally. Brush ducks with wine mixture. Bake
until ducks are deep golden brown, about 1 1/4 hours for
large ducks, 45 minutes for smaller ducks, brushing with
wine mixture occasionally.

While ducks are baking, prepare sauce. In medium
saucepan, blend vinegar and cornstarch. Blend in reserved
broth and remaining sauce ingredients. Heat to boiling
over medium-high heat, stirring constantly. Boil 1 minute.
Serve sauce with ducks and rice.

*Serving Suggestion: If desired, set cooked ducks aside to cool
slightly. Remove rice stuffing from ducks; add to rice mixture in
baking pan, or combine on serving platter. Slice breast and thigh
meat from ducks. Arrange over rice mixture.*

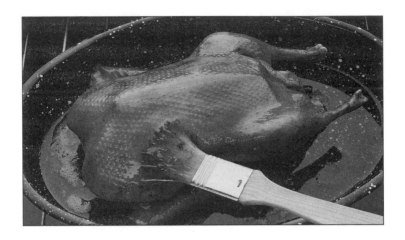

ROAST LEMON-MINT DUCK

   1 whole mallard or other large wild duck,
      skin on
   1 tablespoon finely chopped fresh mint
      Grated rind and juice from one small lemon
   3 tablespoons softened butter, divided
   1/4 teaspoon pepper
   1/8 teaspoon salt
   1 cup duck stock (page 174) or chicken broth
1 1/2 teaspoons finely chopped fresh mint
   1 medium lemon, cut into 6 slices

2 servings

Heat oven to 400°. Pat inside and outside of duck dry with
paper towels. In small bowl, combine 1 tablespoon mint,
lemon rind and juice, and 1 tablespoon butter; mix well.
Rub butter mixture inside cavity. Place duck in 9-inch-
square baking pan. In small saucepan, combine remaining
2 tablespoons butter, the pepper, and salt. Heat over low
heat until butter melts. Brush over outside of duck.

Roast duck until skin is brown and crisp and duck is
desired doneness, 40 to 60 minutes, basting frequently with
pan juices. Transfer duck to heated serving platter. Set aside
and keep warm. Pour pan juices into medium saucepan.
Add stock. Cook over medium heat until reduced by
one-half. Remove from heat. Add 1 1/2 teaspoons mint and
lemon slices. Let stand about 2 minutes. Arrange lemon
slices on duck; pour sauce over lemon slices and duck.

GRILLED TEAL FAST

4 whole teal, skin on
1 whole lemon, quartered
  Olive oil
  Salt and pepper
8 whole juniper berries
4 celery tops with leaves
4 small potatoes
4 small white onions
  Dried oregano leaves, optional

4 servings

Start charcoal briquets in grill. Pat cavities and outsides of ducks dry with paper towels. Rub each duck cavity with one lemon quarter, then with olive oil. Set aside lemon quarters. Sprinkle cavity with salt and pepper. Inside each cavity, place 2 juniper berries, 1 celery top, 1 potato, and 1 onion. Tie drumsticks across cavity with wet kitchen string. Tuck wing tips behind back. Rub outside of each duck with lemon quarter, then with olive oil. Sprinkle with salt, pepper, and oregano.

When charcoal briquets are covered with ash, spread them evenly in grill. Place grate above hot coals. Grill ducks until desired doneness, 15 to 35 minutes, turning once or twice and brushing with olive oil.

TIP: This recipe also works well on a rotisserie.

DUCK BREASTS WITH BACON AND ONIONS

4 boneless breast halves from
  2 wild ducks
1/2 to 1 cup brandy
1/4 cup all-purpose flour
1/4 teaspoon salt
1/8 teaspoon pepper
8 slices bacon, cut up
1 medium onion, very
  coarsely chopped

4 servings

In medium mixing bowl, combine duck breast halves and enough brandy to cover meat. Cover bowl with plastic wrap. Marinate in refrigerator 1 to 2 hours. Drain breast halves; discard brandy. Pat breast halves dry with paper towels. On a sheet of waxed paper, mix flour, salt, and pepper. Dip breast halves in flour, turning to coat. Set aside breast halves. Discard excess flour mixture.

In large skillet, fry bacon over medium heat until crisp. Remove bacon with fork; set aside. Add floured duck breast halves. Fry over medium heat until browned on one side. Turn breast halves over. Add onion. Continue cooking, rearranging breast halves and onions once or twice, until breast halves are desired doneness and onions are tender-crisp. Serve with bacon.

WINE-BRAISED DUCK

1/4 cup all-purpose flour
1/4 teaspoon salt
1/4 teaspoon pepper
2 mallards or other large wild ducks, cut up
2 tablespoons butter or margarine
2 tablespoons vegetable oil
1 medium onion, chopped
2 medium shallots, minced
1 cup red wine
1 cup duck stock (page 174) or chicken broth

8 ounces fresh mushrooms, sliced
1 small bay leaf
1 teaspoon dried thyme leaves
1 teaspoon dried rosemary leaves
1 tablespoon snipped fresh parsley
3 tablespoons cold water
2 tablespoons all-purpose flour
Salt and pepper

4 or 5 servings

On a sheet of waxed paper, mix 1/4 cup flour, the salt, and pepper. Dip duck pieces in flour, turning to coat. In Dutch oven, melt butter in oil over medium heat. Add duck pieces; brown on all sides. Remove duck pieces with slotted spoon; set aside.

Add onion and shallots to Dutch oven. Cook and stir over medium heat until tender. Return duck pieces to Dutch oven. Add wine, stock, mushrooms, bay leaf, thyme, rosemary, and parsley. Heat to boiling. Reduce heat; cover. Simmer until duck pieces are tender, 1 to 1 3/4 hours. With slotted spoon, transfer duck pieces to heated serving platter. Set aside and keep warm. Remove and discard bay leaf. Skim excess fat from cooking liquid. In small bowl, blend water and 2 tablespoons flour. Blend into cooking liquid. Cook over medium heat, stirring constantly, until thickened and bubbly. Season with salt and pepper to taste. Serve sauce over duck pieces.

DUCK IN CORN BREAD STUFFING

Follow recipe on page 144 for Doves in Corn Bread Stuffing, except substitute 2 wild duck breasts, skinned, boned, and cut into 3/4-inch strips, for doves. Proceed as directed. Bake for 1 hour.

DUCK-BREAST RUMAKI

2 boneless breast halves from 1 wild duck
1/2 cup sake or dry sherry
1 tablespoon soy sauce
1 tablespoon peanut oil
1 teaspoon minced fresh gingerroot, optional
8 to 10 slices bacon, cut in half
16 to 20 canned whole water chestnuts

16 to 20 appetizers

Cut each breast half into 8 to 10 pieces, about 1 inch across each. In small mixing bowl, blend sake, soy sauce, oil, and gingerroot. Add duck pieces; stir to coat. Marinate at room temperature for up to 1 hour. Place one duck chunk and one water chestnut on a piece of bacon. Wrap bacon around duck and water chestnut. Secure with toothpick. Repeat with remaining ingredients. Heat oven to broil and/or 550°. Arrange appetizers on broiler pan. Broil 3 to 4 inches from broiler until bacon is just crisp, about 10 minutes, turning once.

SPICY DUCK STIR-FRY WITH PEANUTS

MARINADE:
1 tablespoon soy sauce
1 tablespoon vegetable oil
1 tablespoon cornstarch

SAUCE:
1/4 cup chicken broth or water
2 tablespoons soy sauce
1 tablespoon sherry
2 teaspoons red wine vinegar
1 teaspoon cornstarch

1 large wild duck breast or
  2 smaller wild duck breasts,
  skinned and boned
1 teaspoon sugar
1/2 teaspoon sesame oil
2 tablespoons vegetable oil
2 tablespoons minced fresh
  gingerroot
1/4 to 1/2 teaspoon crushed red
  pepper flakes
1/2 cup salted peanuts
1/4 cup sliced green onions
Hot cooked rice

2 or 3 servings

Cut duck breast into 3/4-inch pieces. In small mixing bowl, blend all marinade ingredients. Add duck pieces. Stir to coat. Refrigerate 30 to 60 minutes.

In small mixing bowl, blend all sauce ingredients. Set aside. In wok or medium skillet, heat 2 tablespoons oil over medium-high heat. Add gingerroot and pepper flakes. Stir-fry about 30 seconds. Add duck mixture. Stir-fry just until duck is firm. Add peanuts. Stir-fry until golden, about 45 seconds. Add sauce and green onions. Stir-fry until thickened and translucent. Serve with hot cooked rice.

MISSISSIPPI DUCK GUMBO

BROTH:
4 or 5 widgeon or other
    medium wild ducks,
    skinned or skin on
1 medium onion, cut up
2 carrots, cut into 2-inch pieces
1/3 cup snipped fresh parsley,
    optional
1 bay leaf
1 to 2 quarts water

ROUX:
3/4 cup vegetable oil
3/4 cup all-purpose flour

6 medium onions, finely
    chopped
3 medium green peppers,
    finely chopped

2 cups finely chopped celery
3 cloves garlic, minced
1 can (28 ounces) whole
    tomatoes, drained and
    cut up
1 to 2 tablespoons
    Worcestershire sauce
1 tablespoon plus 1 1/2
    teaspoons salt
1 1/2 to 2 teaspoons pepper
1/2 teaspoon dried oregano
    leaves
1/2 teaspoon dried thyme leaves
1 package (10 ounces) frozen
    okra cuts
Hot cooked rice

About 4 quarts

In large stockpot, combine all broth ingredients, adding enough water to cover ducks. Heat to boiling. Reduce heat; cover. Simmer until ducks are tender, 1 to 1 1/2 hours. Remove ducks. Strain and reserve broth; discard vegetables. Remove duck meat from bones. Cut meat into bite-sized pieces; set aside. Discard skin and bones. Skim broth; strain through several layers of cheesecloth. Measure 1 quart broth; set aside. Reserve any remaining broth for use in other recipes.

In large stockpot, heat oil over medium heat. Blend in flour. Cook, stirring constantly, until deep golden brown, about 30 minutes. Carefully stir in onions, green pepper, celery, and garlic. Cook, stirring constantly, until vegetables are tender. Stir in duck meat, reserved broth, and remaining ingredients except okra and rice. Heat just to boiling, stirring occasionally. Reduce heat. Simmer, uncovered, for about 30 minutes, stirring occasionally. Add okra. Stir to break apart. Simmer 30 minutes. Serve over hot cooked rice.

Variation: For easier gumbo, cook ducks in pressure cooker as directed on pages 159–160, or use 4 cups leftover cooked duck, goose, or turkey. Use 1 quart duck stock (page 174) or ready-to-serve chicken broth. Prepare flour-oil roux as described above. Continue as directed.

6

• • • • • • • • • • • • • • • • •

STUFFING, GAME STOCK, SAUCES & MARINADES

Stuffing Recipes

Upland game birds and waterfowl should be stuffed just before roasting. Pack the stuffing in lightly, allowing room for expansion.

Both of the recipes in this section make about 5 cups stuffing — enough for a whole goose or turkey, or four pheasants or ducks. Stuffing can also be baked separately as a side dish to accompany roasts, grilled meats, or other main courses. Place it in a greased 1½-quart casserole. Bake, covered, at 350° for 30 minutes. Uncover, and continue baking until the stuffing is hot, 15 to 25 minutes. If you are baking stuffing as a side dish to accompany a roast, spoon pan juices from the roast over the stuffing several times to add flavor.

ONION-BREAD DRESSING LOW-FAT

  1 medium onion, cut in half lengthwise and thinly sliced
¼ cup butter or margarine
4½ cups herb-seasoned croutons
  2 teaspoons dried parsley flakes
½ teaspoon salt
½ teaspoon dried crushed sage leaves, optional
½ teaspoon dried basil leaves
¼ teaspoon dried marjoram leaves
  1 cup game bird stock (page 174) or chicken broth
  1 egg

In medium skillet, cook and stir onion in butter over medium heat until tender. Remove from heat; set aside. In medium mixing bowl, combine croutons, parsley, salt, sage, basil, and marjoram; mix well. Stir in onions and butter. In small mixing bowl, blend stock and egg. Add to crouton mixture; mix well.

APRICOT STUFFING

7 or 8 slices whole wheat or white bread (or half whole wheat, half white bread)
1/2 cup cut-up dried apricots
1/2 cup chopped pecans or walnuts
1 teaspoon dried crushed sage leaves
1 teaspoon dried parsley flakes
1/2 teaspoon salt
1/4 teaspoon pepper
1 medium onion, chopped
1 cup chopped celery
1/4 cup butter or margarine
1 cup game bird stock (page 174) or chicken broth

Heat oven to 325°. Place bread directly on oven rack. Bake until bread is dry, 5 to 10 minutes. Cool. Cut into 1/2-inch cubes; there should be about 5 cups bread cubes. Place bread cubes in medium mixing bowl. Add apricots, pecans, sage, parsley, salt, and pepper. Mix well; set aside.

In medium skillet, cook and stir onion and celery in butter over medium heat until tender. Stir into bread-cube mixture. Add stock; mix well.

NOTE: For moister stuffing, or if stuffing is to be cooked separately, add 1 beaten egg with stock.

Game Stock

Good stock is fundamental to good cooking. It's used as the base for sauces, and as the cooking liquid in many recipes. Game stock is made by boiling the bones of big-game animals, birds, or small game, usually with vegetables and seasonings. It adds more flavor to recipes than commercial chicken or beef broth. For convenience, freeze stock in 1-cup batches or can it in a pressure cooker. Leave 1/2 inch head space in pint jars; process at 10 pounds pressure for 20 minutes.

If you make a large batch of stock, you may want to try a technique used by professional chefs. Prepare the stock without adding salt, then strain it through a double thickness of cheesecloth. Allow the strained stock to cool completely, then skim off any fat. Boil the strained, skimmed stock until it is reduced by half to make a *demi-glace* (half glaze), which is the base for many classic French sauces. Reducing the demi-glace even further produces a hard, rubbery glaze that can be cut into small chunks and frozen. A small chunk of the glaze added to a sauce or braising liquid intensifies the flavor of the dish without adding liquid. If a recipe calls for a teaspoon of instant bouillon granules, you can substitute a small chunk of glaze and a bit of salt.

GAME BIRD STOCK
(Pheasant, Partridge, Grouse, Turkey, or Waterfowl)

1½ to 2 pounds uncooked game bird backs and bones
　1 small onion, quartered
　1 stalk celery, cut into 1-inch pieces
　1 carrot, cut into 1-inch pieces
　¼ cup snipped fresh parsley
　½ teaspoon dried marjoram leaves
　½ teaspoon dried thyme leaves
　6 whole black peppercorns
　2 whole cloves
　1 bay leaf
1¼ teaspoons salt, optional
　4 to 6 cups cold water

About 3 cups stock

In large saucepan, combine all ingredients, adding enough water to completely cover the bones and vegetables. Heat to boiling over medium-high heat. Reduce heat. Skim foam from top of stock. Simmer for 1½ to 2 hours, skimming periodically. Strain through a double thickness of cheesecloth. Discard bones and vegetables. Cool stock slightly. Refrigerate overnight. Skim any solidified fat from top.

RABBIT STOCK

Follow recipe above, substituting 1½ to 2 pounds rabbit backs, ribs, and other bones for the game bird bones. Continue as directed, cooking 2 to 2½ hours.

VENISON STOCK

   Enough deer, antelope, elk, or moose bones to fit stockpot
     (5 to 10 pounds)
4 to 6 carrots, cut into 2-inch pieces
3 or 4 stalks celery, cut into 2-inch pieces
2 medium onions, cut into quarters
2 bay leaves
10 whole black peppercorns
4 or 5 sprigs fresh parsley
1 sprig fresh thyme, or 1/2 teaspoon dried thyme leaves

About 3 quarts

Heat oven to 450°. Arrange bones in roasting pan. Roast
until well browned, about 1 hour, turning bones once during roasting. Transfer bones to stock pot.

Loosen browned bits from roaster by stirring, adding 1
cup water if necessary. Pour liquid into large measuring
cup. Skim fat; discard. Add liquid to stockpot.

Add remaining ingredients to stockpot. Cover bones with
cold water. Heat to boiling over medium-high heat.
Reduce heat. Skim foam from top of stock. Simmer for
about 8 hours, skimming periodically and adding additional
water as necessary to keep bones covered.

Strain stock through a double thickness of cheesecloth.
Discard bones and vegetables. Pour stock back into stockpot. Heat to boiling over medium-high heat. Cook until
reduced to about 3 quarts. Cool slightly. Refrigerate
overnight. Skim any solidified fat from top.

Sauces & Marinades

Sauces enhance the flavor of simply prepared game. Game stock is ideal for use in the sauce recipes on these pages that call for stock. If you substitute prepared beef broth for the game stock, you may wish to reduce the amount of salt in the recipe.

Marinades tenderize tougher cuts of game and add flavor. Most marinades are combinations of oil and an acidic ingredient such as lemon juice, wine, or vinegar, with herbs and spices added for flavor. Experiment with different seasoning combinations to create your own "house blend."

ITALIAN GREEN SAUCE
This sauce is often served in Italy with grilled meats. It's good with any type of game.

1/4 cup soft bread crumbs
2 teaspoons white vinegar
1 hard-cooked egg yolk, chopped
1 or 2 anchovy fillets, cut up, optional
2 teaspoons capers
3/4 cup snipped fresh parsley
2 teaspoons finely chopped onion
1 clove garlic, minced
1/3 to 1/2 cup olive oil

About 3/4 cup

In small mixing bowl, combine bread crumbs and vinegar; mix well. Let stand 10 minutes. In another small bowl, combine egg yolk, anchovy fillets, and capers. Mash with a fork. Add yolk mixture, parsley, onion, and garlic to bread crumb mixture; mix well. Blend in oil until sauce is desired consistency. Let stand at room temperature for at least 30 minutes before serving. Stir before serving. Serve sauce at room temperature.

NOTE: For a smoother consistency, combine all ingredients in blender or food processor. Process just until smooth. Sauce prepared in blender may be served immediately.

DRIED MUSHROOM SAUCE

Serve this sauce with birds or small game. Create your own sauce variations by adding fresh herbs.

1/2 ounce dried morels or other mushrooms (about 2/3 cup)
1 cup warm water
2 tablespoons butter or margarine
2 tablespoons all-purpose flour
1/4 teaspoon salt
Dash white pepper
Dash ground nutmeg
1/4 cup whipping cream or half-and-half

About 1 1/2 cups

Break dried mushrooms into pieces. In small mixing bowl, combine mushrooms and water; stir. Let rehydrate 15 minutes. Remove mushrooms with slotted spoon; set aside. Reserve 3/4 cup soaking liquid.

In small saucepan, melt butter over medium-low heat. Stir in flour, salt, pepper, and nutmeg. Blend in cream, and reserved mushrooms and liquid. Cook over medium heat until thickened and bubbly, 5 to 7 minutes. Serve sauce warm.

MADEIRA GAME SAUCE

Excellent with any big-game roast or steaks.

3 tablespoons butter or margarine
3 tablespoons all-purpose flour
1 cup venison stock (page 175) or beef broth
2 tablespoons currant jelly
2 tablespoons Madeira wine

About 1 cup

In small saucepan, melt butter over medium-low heat. Stir in flour. Blend in stock. Cook over medium heat until thickened and bubbly, 5 to 7 minutes. Add jelly; stir until melted. Add Madeira; heat just to boiling. Serve sauce warm.

BIG-GAME BROWN SAUCE

In classic French cooking, many sauces are based on brown sauce, made by reducing rich stock. The following recipes are variations on that idea, simplified for the home cook.

1/3 cup finely chopped onion
 1 small carrot, finely chopped
 3 tablespoons butter or margarine
1/4 cup dry white wine
 2 tablespoons all-purpose flour
 1 cup venison stock (page 175) or beef broth
 1 teaspoon lemon juice or vinegar
    Salt and freshly ground black pepper

About 1 cup

In medium skillet, cook and stir onion and carrot in butter over medium heat until tender. Stir in wine. Cook, stirring occasionally, until reduced by half. Stir in flour. Blend in stock and lemon juice. Cook over medium-high heat, stirring constantly, until thickened and bubbly, 5 to 7 minutes. Strain sauce if desired. Add salt and pepper to taste. Serve warm.

Richer Big-Game Brown Sauce: Cook onion and carrot in butter as directed in recipe for Big-Game Brown Sauce. Blend in wine; reduce as directed. Stir in flour. Blend in 3/4 cup reduced venison stock (demi-glace, pages 173-174), 1/4 cup white wine, and lemon juice. Cook over medium-high heat, stirring constantly, until thickened and bubbly, 5 to 7 minutes. Strain sauce if desired. Add salt and pepper to taste. Serve warm.

Quick and Easy Big-Game Brown Sauce: Cook onion and carrot in butter as directed in recipe for Big-Game Brown Sauce. Blend in wine; reduce as directed. Omit flour. In small bowl, blend 1 package (.87 ounces) brown gravy mix and 1 cup water. Blend gravy mixture and lemon juice into onion mixture. Cook over medium-high heat, stirring constantly, until thickened and bubbly, 5 to 7 minutes. Strain sauce if desired. If necessary, add salt and pepper to taste. Serve warm.

LEMON-GARLIC MARINADE
This marinade is especially good with upland game birds.

1/2 cup fresh lemon juice
1/2 cup olive oil or vegetable oil
 2 teaspoons dried oregano leaves
 1 teaspoon prepared Dijon-style mustard
 3 cloves garlic, minced
1/8 teaspoon freshly ground black pepper

In small saucepan, combine all ingredients. Heat until bubbly. Cool to room temperature. Marinate game birds or meat at least 3 hours, or overnight, turning occasionally, before grilling or broiling.

GREEK-STYLE MARINADE
Try marinating big-game steaks in this blend before grilling. This is also excellent with ducks.

1/2 cup olive oil or vegetable oil
1/2 cup sweet vermouth
 1 tablespoon lemon juice
3/4 teaspoon dried tarragon leaves
 1 small red onion, thinly sliced and separated
    into rings
1/8 teaspoon cracked black pepper

In small saucepan, combine all ingredients. Heat until bubbly. Cool to room temperature. Marinate game birds or meat at least 3 hours, or overnight, turning occasionally, before grilling or broiling.

Nutritional Chart

If a recipe has a range of servings, the data below applies to the greater number of servings. If the recipe lists a quantity range for an ingredient, the average was used to calculate the nutritional data. If alternate ingredients are listed, the analysis applies to the first ingredient listed, with one exception: canned broth was used in place of homemade stock. Sauces and optional ingredients are not included in the analysis. Data for pheasant was used in all recipes calling for grouse, partridge, or woodcock. Data for squab was used in recipes calling for dove.

	Calories	Fat (g)	Sodium (mg)	Protein (g)	Carbohydrate (g)	Cholesterol (mg)
Apricot Stuffing (1/2 c.) *Exchanges*: 1 S; 1/2 Fr; 1/2 V; 2 F	156	9	390	3	17	10
Baked Pheasant in Madeira *Exchanges*: 8 LM; 1 C; 1/2 V	513	24	540	57	14	175
Barbecued Partridge on Rotisserie (1 bird) *Exchanges*: 111/2 LM; 21/2 C	765	33	660	79	32	245
Bear Steak Flamade *Exchanges*: 1/2 S; 3 LM; 11/2 V; 3 F	373	24	410	25	13	30
Bear Stew *Exchanges*: 1 S; 31/2 LM; 1 V; 1 F	348	16	530	29	21	0
Big-Game Baked Round Steak *Exchanges*: 1/2 S; 5 VLM; 1/2 C; 2 F	292	11	780	34	12	130
Big Game Belgium *Exchanges*: 1/2 S; 71/2 VLM; 1 C; 11/2 V; 81/2 F	753	46	830	56	24	175
Big-Game Pie *Exchanges*: 3 S; 11/2 VLM; 1 V; 6 F	554	33	770	20	44	75
Big-Game Pot Roast *Exchanges*: 1/2 S; 61/2 VLM; 3 V; 2 F	422	13	760	51	23	180
Big-Game Swiss Steak *Exchanges*: 1/2 S; 31/2 VLM; 1 V; 11/2 F	249	9	790	28	13	100
Big-Game Brown Sauce (1 Tbsp.) *Exchanges*: 1/2 V; 1/2 F	29	2	75	.3	1	5

Dietary Exchanges: S=Starch FR=Fruit C=Carb/Other V=Vegetable M=Milk (whole)
F=Fat VLM=Very Lean Meat LM=Lean Meat MFM=Medium-Fat Meat HFM=High-Fat Meat

	Calories	Fat (g)	Sodium (mg)	Protein (g)	Carbohydrate (g)	Cholesterol (mg)
Brunswick Stew *Exchanges*: 1¹/2 S; 3¹/2 VLM; 1¹/2 V; 1¹/2 F	336	11	670	31	29	110
Chicken-Fried Venison Steaks *Exchanges*: 1 S; 5 VLM; ¹/2 M; 3 F	411	21	630	39	16	200
Doves in Corn Bread Stuffing *Exchanges*: 3¹/2 S; 2 LM; 5¹/2 F	621	35	1,460	24	53	110
Dried Mushroom Sauce (1 Tbsp.) *Exchanges*: ¹/2 F	21	2	35	.2	1	5
Duck Breasts with Bacon and Onions *Exchanges*: 2¹/2 MFM; ¹/2 F	607	48	500	30	8	145
Duck in Corn Bread Stuffing *Exchanges*: 3¹/2 S; 2 VLM; 3 F	475	18	1,460	25	53	95
Duck-Breast Rumaki *Exchanges*: ¹/2 S; 4 MFM; 1 V; 5¹/2 F	110	9	140	4	1	20
Elk Tenderloin Sauté * *Exchanges*: ¹/2 S; 3¹/2 VLM; 2 V; 2 F	289	11	1,150	30	16	75
Fillet of Venison (5.25 oz.) *Exchanges*: 5 VLM; 1¹/2 F	227	9	105	35	0	135
Florentine Rabbit Pasta *Exchanges*: 2 S; 3 VLM; 7 F	650	37	210	26	53	175
Fried Deer Heart Slices	Nutritional information not available					
Garlic Sausage (4 oz.) *Exchanges*: 2¹/2 VLM; 2 F	181	11	640	19	.4	70
Grilled Loin with Brown Sugar Baste *Exchanges*: 5 VLM; ¹/3 C; 1 F	233	7	440	34	5	135
Grilled Marinated Pheasants *Exchanges*: 12 LM; 2¹/2 F	788	47	160	83	2	260
Grilled Teal *Exchanges*: 1¹/2 S; 2 LM; ¹/2 V; 3¹/2 F	377	25	60	16	25	60
Hasenpfeffer *Exchanges*: ¹/2 S; 5¹/2 VLM; 1¹/2 V; 4¹/2 F	454	25	680	41	14	170
Homesteaders' Rabbit or Squirrel w/ Cream Gravy *Exchanges*: ¹/2 S; 6¹/2 VLM; 1¹/2 V; 4¹/2 F	489	27	840	49	11	205
Hungarian Huns *Exchanges*: 1 S; ¹/2 Fr; 6¹/2 LM; 2 V; 2 F	574	29	500	52	25	155
Hunter's Favorite Chili *Exchanges*: 1¹/2 S; 4 VLM; 2 V; 5¹/2 F	528	30	950	34	30	125
Italian Green Sauce (1 Tbsp.) *Exchanges*: 2 F	77	8	30	.4	1	20

* Rice, noodles, or toast not included in analysis.

181

	Calories	Fat (g)	Sodium (mg)	Protein (g)	Carbohydrate (g)	Cholesterol (mg)
Italian Meatballs and Sauce* *Exchanges:* 1 S; 2 VLM; 3½ V; 5½ F	492	31	1,640	21	33	105
Madeira Game Sauce (1 Tbsp.) *Exchanges:* ½ S; ½ F	35	2	75	.3	3	5
Mexican Chorizo Sausage (4 oz.) *Exchanges:* 3½ VLM; 2 F	209	12	500	23	1	90
Mexican Enchilada Casserole *Exchanges:* 1 S; 3 VLM; 1½ V; 6 F	448	31	730	26	17	110
Mississippi Duck Gumbo* *Exchanges:* 4½ LM; 1 C; ½ V; 4 F	219	13	800	10	17	30
Old-Fashioned Venison Stew *Exchanges:* ½ S; 4 VLM; ½ C; 4 V; 1½ F	350	9	490	35	30	120
Onion-Bread Dressing *Exchanges:* 1 S; ½ V; 2 F	142	9	490	3	13	35
Orange Onion Liver	Nutritional information not available					
Oriental-Style Grilled Venison Ribs *Exchanges:* 5 VLM; ½ C; 1 F	233	7	520	34	7	125
Oven-Barbecued Rabbit *Exchanges:* 6 VLM; 1 C; 4 V; 2 F	439	13	870	48	33	195
Oven-Barbecued Venison Ribs *Exchanges:* 5 VLM; 1½ C; ½ F	268	4	1,090	35	23	125
Peppered Antelope Roast (4 oz.) *Exchanges:* 4 VLM; 2 F	208	10	150	27	.1	115
Pheasant in Creamy Mushroom Sauce *Exchanges:* 1 S; 8 LM; 1½ V; 3 F	681	40	920	59	17	185
Pheasant Paprika* *Exchanges:* 1 S; 6 LM; 6 F	680	48	1,170	44	16	170
"Poached" Wild Goose *Exchanges:* 7 MFM; 2 F	589	43	150	48	0	175
Polynesian Roast Duck *Exchanges:* 1½ S; 1 Fr; 3½ LM; 1½ C; ½ V; 3 F	556	24	670	27	56	110
Potato Sausage (4 oz.) *Exchanges:* 1 S; 1½ VLM; 1 F	156	6	480	13	11	60
Quail Grilled in Cabbage Leaves *Exchanges:* 7 LM; 1 V; 8 F	777	61	460	51	5	275
Quail in Corn Bread Stuffing *Exchanges:* 3½ S; 5 LM; 4 F	734	37	1,520	45	53	175
Rabbit Braised with Bacon and Mushrooms *Exchanges:* 1 S; 7 VLM; ½ Fr; 1 V; 5 F	579	28	1,010	54	24	215

Dietary Exchanges: S=Starch   FR=Fruit   C=Carb/Other   V=Vegetable   M=Milk (whole)
F=Fat   VLM=Very Lean Meat   LM=Lean Meat   MFM=Medium-Fat Meat   HFM=High-Fat Meat

	Calories	Fat (g)	Sodium (mg)	Protein (g)	Carbohydrate (g)	Cholesterol (mg)
Rabbit in Apple Cider *Exchanges*: 6¹/2 VLM; 2 Fr; 2 V; 2 F	472	14	550	48	39	180
Rabbit or Squirrel Pot Pie *Exchanges*: 2 S; 3 VLM; ¹/2 V; 6 F	518	32	330	27	31	150
Rabbit Stew *Exchanges*: 5¹/2 VLM; 5¹/2 V; 5 F	557	28	1,240	50	27	170
Roast Big-Game Tenderloin (4 oz.) *Exchanges*: ¹/2 S; 2¹/2 VLM; 1 F	143	6	160	16	5	45
Roast Boneless Sirloin Tip (4 oz.) *Exchanges*: 3¹/2 VLM; 1 F	159	5	60	26	0	100
Roast Goose with Baked Apples *Exchanges*: ¹/2 S; 1¹/2 Fr; 1 C; 7 MFM; 2 F	752	45	240	49	38	180
Roast Lemon-Mint Duck *Exchanges*: ¹/2 Fr; 5 LM; 6¹/2 F	582	47	930	35	8	200
Roast Wild Turkey (¹/8 recipe using 12-lb. bird) *Exchanges*: 15¹/2 VLM; ¹/2 V; 6 F	831	38	320	110	5	325
Rolled Stuffed Roast of Venison *Exchanges*: ¹/2 S; 6¹/2 VLM; ¹/2 V; 2 F	341	12	430	48	6	175
Savory Pineapple-Baked Quail *Exchanges*: 2 Fr; 7 LM; 2 F	587	31	220	50	27	190
Savory Pot Pie *Exchanges*: 2 S; 3 VLM; ¹/2 V; 6 F	515	33	350	24	31	120
Sharptail on Mushroom Toast *Exchanges*: 1 S; 3¹/2 LM; 1 V; 4¹/2 F	503	32	610	30	20	125
Sherried Squirrel or Rabbit *Exchanges*: ¹/2 S; 6¹/2 VLM; ¹/2 C; ¹/2 V; 2¹/2 F	385	16	1,280	47	9	185
Skillet Game Hash *Exchanges*: 2 S; 2 VLM; 1¹/2 F	248	9	360	18	24	60
Southern Fried Squirrel or Rabbit with Gravy *Exchanges*: 1¹/2 S; 7 VLM; 5 F	567	29	660	51	22	190
Spicy Duck Stir-Fry with Peanuts* *Exchanges*: ¹/2 MFM; ¹/2 V; 1¹/2 F	477	32	1,390	33	14	100
Spicy Elk Kabobs *Exchanges*: 3¹/2 VLM; 1 V; ¹/2 F	161	3.5	280	27	4	60
Stewed Partridge with Sage Dumplings *Exchanges*: 2 S; 4¹/2 VLM; 2 V; 2 F	433	13	1,300	41	37	120
Stuffed Breasts of Grouse *Exchanges*: 2 S; 4¹/2 VLM; ¹/2 V; 5¹/2 F	579	32	1,520	38	33	170

* Rice, noodles, or toast not included in analysis.

	Calories	Fat (g)	Sodium (mg)	Protein (g)	Carbohydrate (g)	Cholesterol (mg)
Stuffed Roast Goose *Exchanges*: 3 S; 1 Fr; 5¹/2 MFM; 3 F	837	43	520	48	56	165
Sunday Roast Grouse with Dressing	(see Sunday Roast Pheasant with Dressing)					
Sunday Roast Partridge with Dressing	(see Sunday Roast Pheasant with Dressing)					
Sunday Roast Pheasant with Dressing *Exchanges*: 2¹/2 S; 6 LM; 1 V; 5¹/2 F	777	45	1,750	51	38	230
Sweet Italian Sausage (4 oz.) *Exchanges*: 3¹/2 VLM; 2 F	207	12	540	23	1	90
Texas-Style Venison Chili* *Exchanges*: ¹/2 S; 2 VLM; 2¹/2 V; 1 F	196	6	340	19	17	65
Turkey Lentil Soup *Exchanges*: 1 S; 2 VLM; ¹/2 V; ¹/2 F	144	3	870	16	14	25
Tuscan Hare with Pasta*† *Exchanges*: 5 VLM; 3 V; 3 F	364	16	1,110	39	16	135
Upland Birds in Oven Cooking Bag *Exchanges*: ¹/2 Fr; 8 LM; 2 F	585	34	220	56	10	205
Upland Stir-Fry* *Exchanges*: 1 S; 2 VLM; 1 V; 3 F	313	16	660	21	20	115
Venison and Beans *Exchanges*: 2 S; 2¹/2 VLM; ¹/2 C; 3 F	376	18	880	21	36	70
Venison Breakfast Sausage (4 oz.) *Exchanges*: 3 VLM; 3¹/2 F	250	18	520	20	.2	85
Venison Heart Roast	Nutritional information not available					
Venison Meatball Pot Pie *Exchanges*: 3 S; 2 VLM; 6¹/2 F	572	35	1,050	22	45	105
Venison Meatloaf Supreme *Exchanges*: ¹/2 S; 3 VLM; 1 V; 4¹/2 F	362	25	490	24	8	155
Venison Picatta *Exchanges*: 1 S; 5 VLM; ¹/2 C; ¹/2 M; 3 F	407	17	660	37	17	160
Venison Roast Burgundy *Exchanges*: 6 VLM; 2 V; ¹/2 F	284	5	260	47	10	170
Venison Vegetable Soup (1 c.) *Exchanges*: ¹/2 S; 1 VLM; 1 V; ¹/2 F	87	2.5	540	9	8	35
Wild Turkey Picatta with Morels *Exchanges*: 1¹/2 S; 10 VLM; ¹/2 M; 3 F	635	24	610	77	24	240
Wine-Braised Duck 1 S; 2 MFM; 1 V; 5 F	483	38	420	21	14	90
Woodcock in Chablis ¹/2 S; 6¹/2 VLM; ¹/2 C; 1 V; 2 F	396	16	700	46	9	150

Dietary Exchanges: S=Starch FR=Fruit C=Carb/Other V=Vegetable M=Milk (whole)
F=Fat VLM=Very Lean Meat LM=Lean Meat MFM=Medium-Fat Meat HFM=High-Fat Meat
* Rice, noodles, or toast not included in analysis. † Analysis uses nutritional information for wild rabbit.

INDEX

–Editor's Note–
The author, Teresa Marrone, enjoys angling, hiking, hunting and foraging for
wild edibles. She lives in Minneapolis, Minnesota, where she works as a writer
and graphic designer. Her other books include *The Seasonal Cabin Cookbook*
and *The Back-Country Kitchen: Camp Cooking for Canoeists, Hikers & Anglers.*